The Peregrination of an Immigrant Kid

Sa se Mwen

THIS IS ME

Mirline DORT

Some names from personal stories have been omitted or altered to respect privacy of individuals.

Copyright © Mirline Dort 2024

All Rights Reserved. No part of this publication may be reproduced, distributed, or transmitted in any form or by any means, including photocopying, recording, or other electronic or mechanical methods, without the prior written permission of the author, except in the case of brief quotations embodied in critical reviews and certain other noncommercial uses permitted by copyright law.

ISBN 979-8-218-53550-6

Credits:
Cover photo/design: Loy Spade
Edits/Publisher: The LoveJoy Publishing Company
Scripture quotations taken from The Holy Bible, King James Version, KJV, are appropriate for usage and are under the guideline usage amount.
Photography: Laurie MacBrown Photography

Printed via AmazonKDP.

Dedication

To my Saving Grace,

My entire life is driven by you. Thanks for being my inspiration.

Love,
Mirline

Acknowledgments

To my parents

Thank you for all the sacrifices you have made for me and my success.
I love you dearly.

To my siblings

Our friendships mean more than you will ever know and
I thank God for you guys every day.

To my friends/sisters in Christ

Thank you Chloe Reddick-Jackson and Tamecia Thompson-Cole for your unwavering support.

To my besties

I love you guys to pieces. Thank you for always being a phone call away no matter the time and helping me to pickup the pieces.

Kendy Pierre

I love our candid and sometimes hard conversations.
I can always count on you for the truth.

CONTENT

DISCLAIMER..3

DEDICATION...4

ACKNOWLEDGMENT...5

CHAPTER 1: BEGINNING OF A LONG JOURNEY..................8

CHAPTER 2: THE PHILOSOPHY..19

CHAPTER 3: BORN WITH RESPONSIBILITY......................29

CHAPTER 4: MY UNSCRIPTED LIFE..................................36

CHAPTER 5: A WORLD BEYOND MY PARENTS..................46

CHAPTER 6: FINDING ME..53

CHAPTER 7: THE ADOPTION PROCESS............................65

CHAPTER 8: I VOLUNTEERED...80

CHAPTER 9: TRANSITIONING...92

CHAPTER 10: KNOWING MY WHY................................100

CHAPTER 11: LIMITATIONS..111

CHAPTER 12: WHAT NOW..118

ABOUT THE AUTHOR...126

Chapter 1:
Beginning of a Long Journey

In many cultures, migration is seen as a symbol of hope. It symbolizes the prospect of building a brighter future and providing better opportunities, especially for their children. As a child of parents who believed in the power of new beginnings, I was born into a world where constant adaptation and change were essential to one's survival.

Like many others, my parents carried a vision filled with aspirations and possibilities. Moving to a new country was more than just a change in geography; it was a leap into opportunities they had never experienced before. I had no idea what my parents had envisioned regarding Haiti's destruction and its future. Fast forward, now I understand why my dad took that leap of faith to uproot his family and move to the United States. Haiti is in a state of absolute peril under the leadership of gangs and violence. Their decision, driven by love and sacrifice, was meant to pave a smoother path for my future. However, the path to this envisioned future was anything but smooth, and they lacked the foresight to understand how it would affect their children. My father, a man of great vision, hope, and dreams, chose to uproot his family from the familiar streets of Haiti to the sprawling unknowns of the United States. I was eleven, a child perched on the cusp of adolescence, unprepared for the seismic shift that was about to unfold in my life. It was a completely different world. The decision to leave was sudden, like a storm without warning. I remember the flurry of packing, the hushed conversations, and the urgency in the air. My father spoke of a better life and opportunities we couldn't fathom, but all I saw was uprooting everything I held dear. Leaving grandparents, cousins, and childhood friends felt like leaving behind a part of myself.

Once upon a time, Haiti was our safe haven. The food, sandy beaches, carefree atmosphere, and hospitality were perfect. Our home in Haiti was more than just a building; it was a cocoon of memories and warmth. The vibrant streets, filled with the rhythmic beats of Kompa music and the tantalizing aroma of griot, were the backdrop of my childhood. Our spacious house, filled with laughter, reflected the life my parents had built. It was here, amidst the tight-knit community and the embrace of our church, that I learned the values of togetherness and faith. I love my heritage and Haitian culture. There is so many things of value about being raised by Haitian parents; for example, their love language is food, and my mom will feed anyone who enters her home. It doesn't matter about the time; their door is always open to anyone in need. My father would give the shirt off his back if it meant helping someone.

A fun fact about many Haitian households is that coffee is always available no matter the time; we love coffee, and even the kids drink coffee. It was like one of the most common beverages and something present in every household. Haiti, as best as I can describe it, felt perfectly warm—a gentle breezed heat that wasn't too intense but inviting enough to make you want to stay. It felt like taking a deep breath of fresh air, as if all your worries and stress were momentarily lifted.

Upon landing in the United States, I was immediately struck by the difference between the two countries. It was a cold, bleak place, with cold streets and a landscape that did not share Haiti's bright, colorful landscape. The crisp, fast-paced language swirled around me unstoppably as if I were in the middle of a wind. I couldn't understand why my dad decided we had to leave everything behind—our home, our family, our church, and the life I loved in Haiti. We had big houses, space, and familiarity. I had my own room, a sanctuary of my own. But when we arrived in America, everything changed. We moved into a cramped two-bedroom apartment, and suddenly, I had to share a room with my two younger sisters. The loss of space and privacy was overwhelming, but it was more than that.

Coming to the United States felt like stepping into a cold, indifferent world that didn't care about who we were or what we had left behind. Life felt harsh and unfamiliar, like I was constantly struggling to survive in a place that didn't welcome me. Saying it was a culture shock doesn't even begin to capture how lost I felt. It was as if I'd been torn from everything that made sense to me, and now I had to figure out how to exist in this foreign place where nothing felt like home. Our new home, a modest two-bedroom apartment, felt constricting and was nothing like the spaciousness of our home in Haiti. The walls, devoid of the laughter and voices of extended family, echoed with a sense of loneliness.

School in America was a world apart, too. Each area of my life was a completely different thing than I had never seen before. I was among friends in Haiti, bonded by shared culture and history. Here, I was "the immigrant kid", my accent a barrier, my heritage a curiosity. As a child, adapting to a new environment is akin to learning a new language without a teacher. The customs, the language, and even the playground games were unfamiliar. School, a place for learning and education, became a battleground of identity. I quickly learned that being different wasn't always celebrated.

A great deal of attention was given to my accent, my clothes, and even my hair. I was frequently ridiculed for them. As a result, bullying became a part of my daily life, a term too mild for the level of torment I endured internally. My colorful Haitian school uniforms were replaced by casual American attire, leaving me even more alienated. I yearned for the comfort of my old school, where the teachers knew me by name and the lessons were taught in a language I could understand.

> In the United States, school, a place for learning and education, became a battleground of identity. I quickly learned that being different wasn't always celebrated.

In Haiti, the concept of a school uniform was a great equalizer. It didn't matter your family's financial situation; in the classroom, we were all the same. But in America, things again were different. The clothing became a symbol of identity and, unfortunately for me, a target for ridicule. Unacquainted with American fashion sensibilities, my parents dressed me in what they considered best: church dresses with tennis shoes. This attire, a norm back home, became my greatest adversary in the halls of my American school. The jeers and taunts were relentless. Kids would circle me, their words sharp and cutting, poking fun at my mismatched outfit and my accent, which was thick with the musicality of Haitian Creole and French. There's a peculiar pain in being mocked for simply being yourself. It became a constant companion during my early years and married into my memories of coming to America. It was a daily battle, one that chipped away at my self-esteem and left me feeling isolated and vulnerable.

Another battleground in my American school was the school cafeteria. In Haiti, the morning meal consists of eggs with plantains, coffee, bread, Haitian spaghetti, and plantain porridge. In the U.S., since cereal and fruit snacks weren't common options, I would often skip school meals and go hungry due to my unfamiliarity with the lunch choices. As trivial as this may seem, for a child trying to adjust to a life where everything is different, it's a big deal, a sign of an ever-changing world.

I tried to shrink myself, to become invisible, but the spotlight of mockery followed me relentlessly. The laughter of my peers echoed in my ears long after the school bell rang, a haunting reminder of my otherness. Even the classroom offered no respite. Teachers, unable to bridge the language gap, often overlooked me. My raised hand was frequently met with an indifferent gaze. My questions were lost in the sea of English that I was yet to master. It was a silent kind of exclusion that made me question my worth and intellect. My parents, who had envisioned a land of opportunity, were unaware of the struggles I faced.

In our household, the language of emotions was seldom spoken, and I bore my burden in silence. One day, I returned home in tears, my emotions finally spilling over the dam of restraint, which was a turning point. Seeing their child in such distress, my parents were forced to confront the reality of my American school experience. Once lively and vibrant, the sight of their daughter, reduced to a shadow of her former self, was a wake-up call. They realized that while providing for my physical needs was crucial, attending to my emotional well-being was equally important. The change didn't happen overnight.

My parents, navigating their own challenges in this new land, were on a steep learning curve. But they tried, in their own way, to bridge the gap. They began to engage more with my school life, trying to learn English and communicate with my teachers. Getting through this new world was like walking through a maze blindfolded. Simple tasks like grocery shopping or visiting the doctor became complex chores marred by language barriers and cultural misunderstandings. My parents, once pillars of the community in Haiti, now worked tirelessly in menial jobs, their qualifications and experience lost in translation.

These experiences, while seemingly trivial to adults, have profound impacts on a child's psyche. It was a lot for me to process. My sense of identity and worth started to slip away, and the overwhelming world of doubt began to take hold. The security of home felt distant when faced with the daily ordeal of fitting in. My creativity, once a vibrant expression of my inner world, became shackled by the chains of insecurity. This burden is especially overwhelming for me. It became the root of numerous issues. At that age, the approval of friends and classmates sometimes meant more than family! My values were changing as I was trying to cope with just being. The struggle went beyond the schoolyard. In their own adaptation battles, my parents often faced cultural and linguistic barriers at home. Their fatigue and frustration, though silent and unspoken, were clearly seen.

Conversations about school became a dance around the darker aspects of my day. The desire to protect them from additional stress muzzled my pleas for help, leaving me to get through the hard times alone. This unspoken struggle continued, shaping my personality and my outlook on life.

Opportunities for friendships were often weighed against the potential of being hurt or misunderstood. My academic performance, once a source of pride, became just another arena where I felt I had to prove my worth.

The shift in environment triggered a shift within me.

The challenges were not just external but internal as well. I grappled with questions of identity, belonging, and purpose. The bright, confident child of Haiti receded, giving way to a teenager who was uncertain and insecure. I missed the communal dinners, the church gatherings, and the sense of being part of something bigger than myself.

In Haiti, I grew up following the rhythm of life and dancing to its familiar ebbs and flows. Suddenly, I felt disoriented and lost in America after being bombarded by unfamiliar sounds and sights. The language barrier was my first formidable opponent. With its intricate grammar and pronunciation, English felt like an unscalable wall separating me from the world around me. In Haiti, Creole and French flowed from my tongue with ease, just as I felt about my identity. In America, every word I uttered was a struggle, met with either confusion or ridicule. Classroom lessons swirled around me like an incomprehensible mist, leaving me feeling isolated in a room full of chatter. I was the 'other,' who didn't fit into the neatly drawn lines of high school cliques. The laughter and whispers followed me like a shadow, a constant reminder that I was different and didn't belong. At home, the situation was no less challenging. In Haitian culture, especially in our household, emotions were like the fine China reserved for special occasions – rarely displayed and kept out of sight. Conversations about feelings, about the struggles of adapting, were unheard of. It was an unspoken rule that one must endure silently. Thus, the turmoil within me remained a silent storm, invisible to the eyes of those I longed to share it with.

The dichotomy of my life was surprising. At school, I was just the Haitian kid. At home, I was expected to be a resilient immigrant, adapting seamlessly. The weight of these expectations was a heavy cloak draped over my shoulders. One I wore with a stoic resignation. The vibrant, carefree spirit of my Haitian childhood was slowly replaced by a cautious, reserved persona molded by the trials of my new environment. Despite these trials, glimmers of hope shined through the darkness just enough to keep me going.

Journaling has always brought me comfort, offering a space to make sense of my thoughts and find peace in putting them down on paper. Expressing my feelings through writing gave me an outlet without breaking Haitian customs and protocol of not expressing emotion because of the perceived notion that it was a sign of weakness. I desperately needed it. The real world was getting too tough, and I needed a space to be real about what I was feeling. The journey was arduous. Each day was a test, a lesson in endurance.

But slowly, I began to find my footing.

I learned the complexities of this new social landscape to find allies in the form of teachers who recognized my struggle and peers who appreciated my uniqueness. The mockery didn't disappear, but my reaction to it evolved. I developed a thicker skin, a sense of humor, and a perspective that allowed me to see beyond the narrow confines of high school hierarchies.

As years passed, the contours of my identity began to take a new shape. I learned to navigate the complexities of my dual heritage, finding strength in my Haitian roots while weaving in the threads of my American experiences. The turning point in my journey of isolation came unexpectedly, a serendipitous twist that brought a glimmer of light into my world. Amidst the sea of unfamiliar faces and voices at school, I met a French student, Noële, whose story mirrored mine in many ways. Like me, her family had moved to the United States to pursue a better life. However, unlike me, she had a firmer grasp of English, a skill that soon became a bridge between my isolated world and the bustling life of the school. Our friendship began with a simple act of kindness. She noticed my struggles in class, how I strained to decipher the teacher's words, and the puzzled look that often clouded my face. One day, she quietly sat next to me and began translating the lessons into French. Noële's words were a great help, guiding me through the fog of confusion and language barriers. I felt a sense of belonging for the first time since I had set foot in the school.

Her assistance went beyond the academic. She became my ally, my guide in this new and perplexing culture. With her help, I began navigating American school life's nuances. She taught me slang, introduced me to American customs, and even gave me tips on how to blend in with my peers. Her presence reminded me that I was not alone in this journey. Our shared experiences created a bond that was more than language and culture. We understood each other's struggles, the silent battles we fought daily, and the longing for a sense of home in a foreign land.

Our conversations, a mix of French, English, and laughter, became the highlight of my school days. She was more than just a friend. She was a lifeline, a connection to a world I was slowly learning to navigate. Gradually, the school, which once felt like a fortress of solitude, became more approachable. Her friendship gave me the courage to interact more with my classmates, participate in class discussions, and engage with the school community. I started to understand the lessons better, not just linguistically but contextually. The sense of accomplishment in comprehending and responding in English was empowering. This confidence had a ripple effect on my life. I began to come out of my shell, embracing the challenges with a newfound strength. The bullying and isolation didn't disappear overnight, but they no longer held the same power over me. I found strength in knowing I had a friend, an ally who shared my story and stood by my side.

Meeting someone who shared a similar story and understood the unspoken complexities of being an immigrant was a turning point. It was a reminder that sometimes, all it takes to change one's world is a single act of kindness, a willingness to reach out and connect. My story of being an immigrant child is not just about overcoming a language barrier but also about how the power of human connection can empower and shift transitional moments in your life. By offering her friendship and compassion at a time when I needed it most I believe was pivotal. As I attempted to fit into a new environment and adapt to a whole new culture, Noelle's understanding and kindness provided a lifeline. At an age when simply navigating daily life was hard enough, her presence made an immeasurable difference, helping me find my footing in a world that often felt overwhelming and alien. Her support gave me the strength to face each day and the confidence to embrace my new reality. I was able to see that even in the lengthy and often intimidating immigration journey, small moments of empathy and solidarity can make all the difference.

Chapter 2:
The Philosophy

    Youth in Haiti often joke about the three places that most teenagers are allowed to visit in Haitian culture; Lekol, Legliz, and Lakay, also known as the 3 L's—School, Church, and Home. As a teenager, it's easy to joke about these being the only places you're ever allowed to go, and honestly, it's not far from the truth. Most Haitian kids laugh about it to keep from crying, but deep down, we know it's just our reality. In this world, the most thrilling adventures you'll ever experience unfold between the pages of textbooks and the four walls of your house. And who needs more than that, right?

    This is the sad truth. The joke, though seemingly benign, holds layers of meaning. On the surface, it is a playful acknowledgment of our sheltered lives. Yet, beneath the humor lies an unspoken acknowledgment of our limitations and constraints. While providing a sense of security and direction, this structured existence also limited our exposure to the world beyond these three realms. My father did not deviate from the philosophy of the 3 L's. If it did not involve church or school, I generally could not even talk about it.

In our circle, the concept of a wild time was mastering the art of sneaking in an extra hour of TV or maybe, just maybe, questioning why trigonometry would ever be relevant in our future lives. Our version of teenage rebellion was so subdued that, looking back, it almost seems quaint, especially when we see it in the light of American culture. But we may not have had frequented parties or discos, but we had fun; the type that comes with deep community ties, shared cultural backgrounds, and familial love that is overbearingly comforting.

Our lives may seem like a repetition of familiar routines—school, church, home—but each of these paths were rich with stories, laughter, and a sense of belonging that only a Haitian teen could truly appreciate. It was a unique blend of tradition, discipline, and a zest for life that kept things interesting. So, as I look back at those days, I see them not as a limitation but as a different kind of adventure. As life oscillated strictly among these three focal points of "L's", school was a given, a place of learning and discipline where we were molded into educated individuals. Church was a mandatory spiritual haven, a weekly pilgrimage where faith and moral teachings were instilled. Our home was our place of familial love, care, and strict oversight.

Our experiences were filtered through the lens of what was deemed appropriate or necessary, leaving little room for exploration or self-discovery outside these boundaries. This sheltered upbringing had its advantages. It instilled a strong sense of discipline, a clear moral compass, and a deep respect for education and faith. We grew up with a firm foundation in the values and traditions of our culture. However, it also meant that we were often ill-prepared for the complexities and nuances of the world outside.

The transition from the simple life in Haiti to life in America laid this lack of preparedness bare. Suddenly, I was thrust into a world that operated on a completely different set of rules and expectations. Here, the freedom and choices available to young people were far broader than anything I had experienced back home. The American way of life, emphasizing individuality and exploration, contrasted with the structured, community-centric life I was used to in Haiti.

> "In the United States, school, a place for learning and education, became a battleground of identity. I quickly learned that being different wasn't always celebrated."

At home, my parents did not play about going to church. Church was the center of our lives. We celebrated, mourned, and sought guidance there. Like clockwork, we dressed in our finest every Sunday and headed to the church, a place as familiar as our home. Our church's towering steeple and wooden pews dominate my childhood memories. "...but as for me and my house, we will serve the Lord." Joshua 24:15 (KJV). This verse was taken quite literally by my parents, to the point where they would threaten to kick my siblings and I out of the house if we dared to utter the words, "I don't want to go to church today." Though I embrace my Haitian culture and my upbringing, the Haitian church is the only aspect I could live without. Most Haitian churches know when to start but not when to end. Growing up, my siblings and I dreaded Sundays because it was an all-day event at church. We went to Sunday school from 8 a.m. to 9:30 a.m., followed by breakfast at the church, and then the main service was from 10:00 a.m. to 1:30 p.m. We would make it home by 3 p.m. because we had to fellowship with everyone we hadn't seen all week. After lunch and dinner at home, we would go back to church for the evening service and wouldn't get back home until around 10 p.m. And unfortunately, if we didn't finish school assignments Friday or Saturday, it had to be done Sunday night before lights out by 10 pm.

At an early age I was baptized. Even though I did not fully understand what being born again meant at the time, I just did what was told and expected of me. But after experiencing so much in life, I now understand the concept, and I'm grateful that my parents encouraged me to make that commitment. These early moments in life planted seeds that would unbeknownst to me later produce vibrant visuals of faith, perseverance and assurance. I've been to some scary places in my life. Whether it was the sandy hot days in Afghanistan or the cold dark nights in Fort Drum, New York, my foundation of faith kept me going. I never felt abandoned by God, even when I was physically alone.

Although I was forced to attend church and dreaded Sundays, it was more than just a place of worship; it was a community center where friendships were forged, and life's milestones were celebrated, as that was the only social gathering we were allowed to attend, even when we moved to America. The vibrant hymns, the passionate sermons, and the communal prayers were the soundtrack of my youth. But as much as the church was a part of me, I felt confined by it. The rituals and routines, deeply ingrained in my family's life felt more like obligations than expressions of faith at times. The church followed us when we moved to America, but it was different; it was not home. In their effort to hold onto a piece of our Haitian heritage, my parents found a church that mirrored the one back home. The sermons were preached in Creole, but they didn't resonate with the struggles of my new life.

Regarding school in America, I encountered peers who had grown up with a level of autonomy I hadn't known. They spoke of weekend outings, hobbies and interests outside the academic and religious spheres. Their ease in navigating social situations, their openness to new experiences, and their ability to articulate their thoughts and opinions were qualities I admired but found hard to emulate. But as for me, away from the watchful eyes of my parents and the close-knit Haitian community, I faced the challenge of forging my path. The safety net of the '3 L's' was no longer there, and I had to learn to navigate life's complexities on my own. Decision-making, time management, and personal responsibility were skills I had to develop on the fly.

Conversations often revolved around school achievements or church teachings. Leisure activities were limited and carefully chosen, ensuring they aligned with the values my father held dear. For this reason, television programs, books, and even friendships were filtered through this lens, creating a bubble that shielded us from external influences he deemed distracting or detrimental. This also meant that many aspects, like popular culture, sex, or leisure activities, that my peers engaged in were alien concepts within our home. My curiosity about these facets of life often went unsatisfied, brushed aside as unnecessary or frivolous in the face of 'more important' matters. The impact of this upbringing became more apparent as I grew older.

Each day, as I walked the halls of my American high school, I was acutely aware of the differences between my peers and I. I often fell silent around my classmates. Their world seemed colorful and very different from mine, one that I had little access to or knowledge of except when I was in their presence. This gap left me out of most social groups, where I was an observer rather than a participant. As I entered adolescence, I yearned to understand and experience the world my peers lived in, which seemed vibrant and exciting, but my father would not allow it. My father's philosophy, though well-intentioned, created an invisible barrier between me and the multifaceted world around me. It was a barrier that I gradually began to push against, seeking a balance between my disciplined upbringing and the diverse experiences I craved. This push for balance was not a rejection of my father's values but an attempt to broaden the scope of my life. Moreover, the high school experiences that my American peers eagerly anticipated and relished, the excitement of dressing up for a dance, the buzz of homecoming week, and the glamour of prom night, were not allowed for me.

    I remember distinctly the first time I mustered the courage to ask my father if I could attend a school dance. The answer was something like this, "You want to dance and get pregnant?" And that was that. Let that sink in. How, as a teenager, did he think that I equated the two by just asking to go to the dance? My father's response was swift and unequivocal. His words, steeped in concern but laced with the strictness I had come to know so well, echoed the fears and values of a typical Haitian parent. His worry about potential negative influences or outcomes overshadowed the idea that a school dance could be a simple, innocent enjoyment. This exclusion was symbolic of the broader cultural divide I navigated daily. I remained silent while my classmates chatted about dance themes, dates, and outfits.

    The depth of this strict reality, as typical of a Haitian child as it was, often felt like a heavy cloak. It was a constant reminder of the duality of my identity – a Haitian girl trying find her place in the American tapestry. This duality was a tightrope walk, where every step was carefully calculated to balance my heritage and the new culture I was immersed in. I vividly recall the first time I got my period, and my father's version of the "sex talk" went something like, "You are a woman now. If a boy touches you, you will get pregnant." There goes that word again.

Pregnant. Fear echoed. His worry about potential negative influences or outcomes overshadowed the lesson he was supposed to teach me about the changes my body would grow through. This was not unexpected. Our Haitian culture forbade anything like sex-ed talk. The idea for a child to learn about or talk about sex in front of adults was frowned upon.

The cultural norm in our Haitian household was to keep emotions subdued to maintain a facade of contentment and compliance. This internal conflict was compounded by the lack of an outlet to express these feelings. This left little room for me to voice my struggles and articulate the sense of being torn between two cultures while dealing with two sets of expectations and two versions of myself. As a teenage girl caught in the currents of two distinct cultures, my life was a study of contrasts and constraints. There was a part of me that longed to dive into the experiences of my American classmates, laugh at their jokes, participate in their activities, and understand their world. And the other part, there stood my father's philosophy, rooted in the traditions of Haiti, holding me in a firm, unyielding grip. This dichotomy left me feeling divided, a traveler perpetually straddling the border of two worlds, belonging fully to neither.

As for my American counterparts, their conversations were peppered with references of popular culture, weekend plans, and teenage milestones, realms that were foreign and inaccessible to me. I observed their ease of interaction, casual confidence, and freedom to express themselves, traits I admired yet felt distant from. The memories of those unattended dances hold a bittersweet place in my heart. They are reminders of the sacrifices and choices that shaped my journey and the cultural nuances I navigated as an immigrant's child.

Although I wouldn't trade my experiences for anything, my father's strict way of life still haunts me after all these years. I can recall even years after living on my own. I would hear my father's voice questioning my actions. I would always ask myself, 'Would my father be okay with this decision?' I often had to remind myself that I no longer needed his approval. It wasn't until later that I was able to reconcile my two cultures and find a balance that allowed me to be true to myself. With time, I realized I could define my timeline, write my own story, and discover the world beyond the boundaries that once seemed impossible.

Fast forward, my relationship with the church changed as I grew older and more independent. Once I left my parents' house, I drifted away from the weekly rituals. Once the obligation was removed, I felt no need to go to church and stayed away for years. The forced attendance of my childhood had built a barrier between me and the faith that was supposed to be its foundation. I needed to discover what faith meant to me outside the confines of my parent's expectations and the church's structure.

This journey of spiritual self-discovery was not rooted in rebellion but a quest for authenticity. I could quote scriptures and sing hymns, but I did not know God for myself. The God that Mom always spoke of, the God of Abraham and Jacob, I had not encountered Him for myself. I was living on my terms with my newfound freedom, and church was not a priority. During this time, I discovered that God relentlessly wanted to love and have a relationship with me. God is omnipotent. He's everywhere. Most people get the confusion that He chases after us, and at one point I felt that was me. But he does not have to chase to prove His love. The biggest exchange of love that I experienced was learning that He was always there. I just had to learn to surrender to Him.

Before I gave my resolved yes to God, I encountered a spectrum of beliefs and practices. Some resonated deeply with me, echoing the core values I had grown up with. In contrast, others challenged my perspectives, pushing me to question and grow. This journey was not just about religion; it was about understanding my place in the world, my connection to a higher power, and the values I chose to live by. Over time, I gradually developed a personal relationship with God, one that was uniquely mine and deeply meaningful. It was not defined by the church's rituals or my parents' expectations but by my experiences, questions answered, and intimate revelations. This personal faith walk was less about attending a particular church and more about how I lived my life, treated others, and understood my purpose. It was less about membership and more about becoming captivated by my Creator.

This path wasn't always easy and there have been situations where it took longer to realize that what I believed retained the answer to it all. And when I lost friends, came close to becoming homeless, and had no one to turn to, God was the only consistent source of strength and love. There is something that happens when you realize that you don't have to do it alone! You don't have to know the next step because you serve a God who knows it all. During these seasons, I discovered Jeremiah 29:11 (KJV) to be truth. " For I know the thoughts that I think toward you, saith the LORD , thoughts of peace, and not of evil, to give you an expected end." That's it. He's got me.

Everything that I've been through in my life, I've made it by the grace of God. There were many times when I didn't see a way out...but God. As I forged this new path, I began to see the value in the foundations laid by my parents. The lessons of compassion, community, and toughness engrained through the teachings and ways of the Haitian church were still a part of who I was. My faith, now a unique blend of my heritage and personal journey, became a source of strength and guidance.

> "But God!" That's the mantra I live by now.

Chapter 3:

Born with Responsibilities

In Haitian culture, being the oldest child meant being born into a world of responsibilities. From the very first breath, those responsibilities intertwined with life itself, weaving a different narrative than the typical childhood tales. This wasn't just about sharing household chores; it was a fundamental part of my identity. While other kids reveled in carefree outdoor play, forming bonds and chasing adventures, my world was laced with duties and expectations. It wasn't about what I wanted to do but what I needed to be done.

No afternoons were spent idly tossing a ball around or exploring the neighborhood with friends. Friendships, leisurely conversations, or after-school activities found no place in my schedule. My time was consumed by a different script that outlined chores, helping out, and looking after my younger siblings. Later in life, having friends or hanging out had a different meaning for me. Because of this, one of the most enjoyable parts of my military life was the friendships I forged. Growing up, I always yearned for this.

It wasn't that I resented these responsibilities; they were simply part of my life and became significant duties that I had to shoulder, as expected. In this cultural landscape, the oldest child was entrusted with ensuring the household ran smoothly. Play and leisure were secondary to the chores in comparison to the obligations that awaited each day. The weight of these responsibilities wasn't measured in pounds or kilograms but in the moments that slipped away, in the experiences I missed while tending to familial needs. However, in those moments, I didn't know what I was losing until I saw other kids being unconcerned about the latter siblings, and they were the responsibility of their parents. This was also a part of the cultural change I witnessed when we moved to the U.S.

There was joy and love in my world; it was just a different shade of hue, one in which responsibility was woven into everything I did. I understood the burden of duty and the importance of selflessness at a young age, but how much can a child truly bear? It was inevitable that, at some point, the child would take on the effects of his environment, which would also be the case for me. I still remember that after the school bell rang, signaling the end of classes, my day was far from over. While other kids scampered off to relish their free time, I stepped into another role, shouldering the responsibilities of being the eldest sibling.

Their laughter, cries, and demands became the backdrop of my after-school hours. Due to the fact that my mother was always ill throughout her pregnancies, I was brought up to be her right-hand woman during those times too, which meant I would ensure dinner was done and my siblings wanted for nothing. The moment I stepped through our front door, I shed the role of a student and embraced the mantle of a second parent.

Homework time for them meant it was my time to step in. Bathing, feeding, ensuring their needs were met, and preparations for the coming day were tasks that fell on my shoulders daily. My younger siblings never stepped foot in a daycare facility. I became their caretaker, guide, and support system. It wasn't a role I sought or volunteered for, but it was one I had to fulfill.

Haitian culture doesn't delineate between parents and older siblings when it comes to nurturing and care. The dynamic of being the eldest child often leads to a selfless dedication to the needs and well-being of younger siblings. While this role embodies responsibility and care, it can gradually erode one's individuality. The focus on meeting the needs of others eclipses personal desires and aspirations, leading to a loss of self amid the continuous giving.

The concept of a fun, playful sibling relationship always seemed like a distant dream to me, especially after moving to America. I would often observe my classmates, their lives enriched with the joy, playfulness, and good company that comes from having siblings. This idealized sibling bond was something I yearned for, but I was far away from this kind of relationship. I would hear them talk about their weekend adventures, the pranks they played on each other, and the secrets they shared. Their stories were filled with laughter, light-hearted arguments, and full-blown battles, but I had nothing of that sort. It was the complete opposite of that.

While I cherished my siblings deeply, our relationship bore the weight of a subtle resentment that often went unnoticed by others. They saw me as an authority figure. This inadvertently distanced us from establishing the typical sibling dynamics. Their perception of me as a quasi-parental figure cast a shadow over our relationship, which sometimes eclipsed the simple joys of being siblings. I longed for moments of unfiltered connection where we could shed the weight of responsibilities and simply be siblings.

I sometimes felt overwhelmed by their dependence on me, but complaining about it was not part of Haitian culture. The pressure to be a role model and get things right often messed with my peace of mind. There were times when it was just too much to handle. I always felt that I had to be perfect and a role model for others, which was a massive burden on my shoulders. It felt like I could not make mistakes. For that reason, I had to figure many things out independently. Forward-thinking, when I got pregnant, it never crossed my mind to turn to my family. Given the situation of having a child out of wedlock, which I will discuss in a later chapter, I knew that it would not suit my position as a role model for my siblings. My parent's faith in me, though innocent, kept me from letting my guard down because I didn't want to disappoint them.

Often misunderstanding, a rift carved by their perception of me and my concealed struggles continued to add pressure to my already complicated navigation of learning who I was. They looked up to me with admiration, seeing in me a figure of confidence and impeccable capability. Yet, behind the facade of composure, it was different being was there. Their obliviousness to the battles I fought within myself deepened the chasm between us. While they believed I effortlessly juggled responsibilities, the reality was a constant tug-of-war between the duty I shouldered and the desire for my own identity. Their innocence shielded them from the storms raging within me. The pressure to be the epitome of perfection in their eyes, to maintain the illusion of a flawless role model, became an unspoken mandate. It wasn't just about living up to parental expectations but about living up to the pedestal my siblings unwittingly placed me upon.

I yearned to tell them about the cracks in the facade, to unravel the layers of complexity beneath the surface. But the fear of disillusionment held me back. Their trust in me was a fragile thread that tethered our relationship, and I feared that revealing my vulnerabilities would shatter that delicate bond. Their belief in the favoritism from our parents added another layer to the pressure cooker of my existence. I grappled with the weight of responsibilities and the perceived notion that their love for me was somehow greater simply because of the roles I played within our family dynamics. Their perception of reality was far from the truth. It wasn't about favoritism but rather the unspoken responsibilities that were thrust upon me as the eldest. It is their innocent misunderstandings that built walls around the truth, keeping them distanced from the reality of my struggles while also widening the gap between our perceptions of our familial roles.

At 19, the walls of our home felt suffocating, the air thick with unspoken obligations and cultural norms that stifled any sense of personal freedom. In Haitian households, the trajectory of life is scripted with certainty. There's an unspoken timeline, a roadmap of our culture. While I grappled with the complexities of growing up in two distinct worlds, my Haitian heritage demanded adherence to its predefined script.

The confinement of the 3Ls was expended when I asked my dad for a cell phone at 16, my junior year in high school. I remember bargaining with my dad about the phone. The rule remained: I cannot have it if it does not benefit school or church. I mustered up some courage to suggest getting a job to pay for it. His response took me by surprise when he agreed. It was because I was expecting a flat "NO" that I couldn't find the words. However, his yes came with restrictions. The work could not interfere with chores. I could not fail any class or receive anything below a C, and my curfew remained at 10 p.m. I eagerly agreed to all these terms. My dad was unaware that I had already spoken to the manager at our local McDonald's, and the manager told me to come back when I turned 16 and that he would work with my school and parents' schedule, so this worked great for me. But see, here's the thing: my father is a hard-working man and believes work equates to freedom, so he was incapable of saying no to me asking to go to work even though he did not want that for me. Whatever his reasoning was, I didn't care. Work meant I had another place to go to. It also meant I would get a cell phone out of the deal. So, all in all, I was happy.

    Being unable to do the typical high school stuff, like dressing up for prom or having sleepovers with friends, stung. Work became an outlet for me. Having a job while living at home gave me the means to prepare to leave home sooner than anticipated. And eventually, it came as a storm. The decision to depart wasn't a mere escape but a calculated step towards a life that resonated with my aspirations. It wasn't about forsaking my heritage or dismissing the values instilled by my parents; it was about finding a balance between cultural heritage and personal freedom. Leaving home at 19 wasn't just about physical distance; it was about reclaiming agency over my own life, about crafting a narrative that echoed my aspirations rather than societal dictates.

    Dating in Haitian Culture is a forbidden territory. However, an unwritten rule suggests that one should be married and ready to have children by 25. The clash between these expectations and the desires that pulsed within me intensified each year. Although I was prohibited from dating or having male friends, I am expected to become a mother and wife by 25.

    The further away from the constant reminder and responsibilities to uphold the cultural norms began to shatter the walls around me as I ventured into the unknown. It wasn't an easy journey as I perceived it to be. Amidst the uncertainties and the unfamiliarity of independence, I found a sense of liberation, a space where I could explore my identity beyond the confines of familial expectations. Although the unspoken rules and expectations faded as I charted my path, my life was very much still impacted. As I transitioned into adulthood, the scars of those early years remained. Decisions were often clouded by the insecurities fostered in those formative years. Personal and professional relationships were approached with a guarded heart, always preparing for the worst, even if it had nothing to do with the decision needing to be made. The dream my parents held for me seemed like a distant echo, overshadowed by the reality of my experiences. The dream of me succeeding and not letting their investment be in vain. Even after I moved out of my parent's house I still yearned for their approval, and I couldn't bear the thought of disappointing them.

Chapter 4:
My Unscripted Life

    The transition from a Haitian childhood to adolescence in the United States was about changing my clothes and hairstyle as much as learning a new language and culture. In school, I was the kid who stood out simply because of my looks, a vivid reflection of my Haitian heritage amid American norms. It's hard to forget the church dresses my mother made me wear to school with tennis shoes. I wore those outfits with pride because they were the norm in Haiti, and I did not stand out because of them. These bright and beautiful dresses were a part of what connected me to my friends in Haiti, but now it was another story. Those dresses became my armor on a battlefield where I stuck out like a sore thumb. Pairing these dresses with tennis shoes, as my parents insisted, only added to my unique appearance. It wasn't the fashion statement I had hoped for in my efforts to blend in.

    Then there was my hair, styled by my mother, who, bless her heart, had one signature look for me. Two big ribbons tied in bows on each side of my head, a row of braids in the back, and two gogo barrettes in the front, a hairstyle that screamed 'different.' This might have been a cute look in Haiti, but it was a beacon that drew teasing and unwanted attention in my American school. My mother was relieved when I started doing my hair. It was her least favorite chore anyway. As I took charge of my hairstyle, she saw it as one less task for her. I experimented with styles, slowly shedding the image of the Haitian girl with ribbons and barrettes and inching closer to the appearance of my American classmates.

My struggle with fitting in was a constant battle throughout the school year. The dresses, the hair, and the entire package were all symbols of where I came from but also barriers to where I was trying to go. Keeping in line with our Protestant values, my parents set strict rules about no pants, no makeup, and only natural hair. Eventually, as they watched me struggle, they too began to adapt, but it took quite some time. They realized that some adjustments were necessary as they grew in understanding of this new world and how it affected their daughter. With each change in my attire and every new hairstyle I tried, I slowly carved out a space where I could be less of an outsider and more just another student.

Making it through the rough seas of bullying and cultural isolation wasn't easy. Each day, I thought I found the key to ignoring the mean comments, the laughter, and the pointed fingers. I put on a brave face, acting as if their words didn't cut deep, even though, in reality, they did. I remember walking through the school corridors, my head held high, pretending to be unfazed by their taunts about my clothes or accent. I was scared to speak up, not just because I didn't want to give them more reasons to make fun of me, but also because I was afraid of stumbling over my English. I feared my language barrier would become another source of ridicule, so I chose silence as my refuge. But silence has its price. It was like bottling emotions inside a pressure cooker, waiting for the lid to blow off. By the time I reached 8th grade, my style - a blend of Haitian tradition and a reluctant nod to American norms was a constant source of internal conflict. My school days were a repetitive cycle of standing out for all the wrong reasons, and each day felt like walking into a battle I was ill-equipped to fight.

    The day it all came to a head is still vivid in my memory. I returned home, a bundle of raw emotions, tears streaming down my face, barely able to get the words out. I was exhausted from trying to be brave, tired of being the odd one out. The bullying had escalated to the point where I couldn't take it anymore. "This is it," I remember telling my parents. "I am not going back to school unless I can dress like the other kids and fix my hair." Seeing me in that state, my mother's heart broke. She understood the depth of my pain, the weight of the struggle I had been carrying. As a mother now, I can understand why my mother's heart was shattered that day. For parents who rarely showed emotion, my outburst was a clear signal that the situation was serious and urgent action was needed.

    My mom became my advocate, gently but firmly persuading my dad that a change was necessary. She knew that convincing him wouldn't be easy, given our strict Christian upbringing where pants, permed hair, and makeup were considered inappropriate. But she also knew that her daughter's happiness and sense of belonging were at stake. I still remember the sheer joy when my mother bought me my first pair of Walmart jeans. It wasn't just about the jeans; it was a symbol of change, stepping closer to fitting in and beginning to bridge the gap between my Haitian roots and my American reality. The feeling was akin to a kid in a candy store but multiplied a hundredfold.

    It was a turning point, not just for me but for my entire

family. It was the moment they realized that while holding onto our cultural values was important, adapting to our new environment was equally crucial for my well-being. From then on, the journey gradually shifted towards finding a middle ground. Though hesitant at first, my parents began to embrace the changes necessary for my adaptation. The transition was not immediate, but each step; a new pair of jeans or a different hairstyle; was a step towards finding my identity in this new world.

    The battle to perm my hair was even tougher. My father, holding firmly to our religious beliefs, was initially opposed to the idea, but as he saw the toll the bullying and my feeling of alienation were taking on me, he began to soften his stance. By the time freshman year rolled around, my parents had come to understand that to help me navigate this new world, they would have to be more lenient. Finding the courage to stand up and voice my needs was something I never thought I had in me. Looking back, I am unsure where that burst of bravery came from. Maybe it was the culmination of all the bullying, the feeling of being an outsider, and the desperate need to belong. Perhaps it was a moment of sheer desperation, a breaking point that pushed me to speak up.

    Stepping into college life was a non-negotiable chapter in my journey, shaped by the deep-rooted expectations of my Haitian heritage. Enrolling in community college, I chose a science major, not just out of personal interest but also as a fulfillment of the unspoken pact between Haitian parents and their children, especially the firstborns. In a Haitian household, the oldest child carries responsibilities that stretch far beyond the confines of the home. We're seen as the torchbearers who must not only uphold the family's honor but also ensure its upward trajectory, especially once you leave.

It's not about what you want....

This expectation comes with a heavy burden, a pressure to succeed that's both motivating and overwhelming. Our parents invest in us, not just financially but emotionally and culturally. And in return, they expect us to invest every ounce of our being into building a successful future. For me, college was more than just a pursuit of education; it was a mission to uphold the sacrifices and dreams my parents carried with them from Haiti. Somewhere along these lines, my pursuit became my own.

Every lecture I attended and every exam taken was a step towards fulfilling that silent promise I made to them. Moving out before achieving a certain level of success wasn't just frowned upon; it was considered a failure and deviation from the path they had so carefully laid out for me. In our culture, the cycle of care and support is a full circle. Haitian parents do not believe in the concept of nursing homes. It's understood, almost written in stone, that the oldest child, especially if she's a daughter, will take care of her aging parents. This responsibility is seen as a sacred duty, an act of giving back to those who gave you everything. The ironic flip side to this was the fierce independence of elderly Haitians further complicates this cultural norm. They cling to their autonomy with a stubbornness that is both admirable and sometimes frustrating. They'll manage on their own until the very end, only relinquishing control when they absolutely have no other choice.

Navigating college with these responsibilities looming in the background was a unique experience. While my peers were planning dorm room decorations or spring break trips, my mind often wandered to future responsibilities.

How would I balance a career with caring for my parents?

How could I ensure that their sacrifices were not in vain?

    Despite these worries, college was also a time of personal growth and exploration. For the first time, I was in an environment where my background was just one part of a diverse tapestry. I met people from different cultures and backgrounds, each with their own stories and expectations. This diversity helped me see my situation from a new perspective. It made me appreciate the depth of my parents' sacrifices and the strength of the cultural values they instilled in me. I had the opportunity to have an experience I had always wanted. I was ready to build a new life out here! The limitations that I experienced for so many years were removed just like that! I felt like a free spirit.
    As I progressed through college, the balance between personal ambitions and familial duties remained a constant theme. The pressure to succeed was always there, but it became a driving force rather than a burden. I learned to embrace it, using it as fuel to propel me forward. Looking back, I realize my college years were crucial in my journey. They were a bridge between the past of my parents and the future I was building for myself.
    Because of the language barrier and communication issues, school was never easy for me in the United States. This class called ESOL (English for Speakers of Other Languages) was a God sent! I found a sense of belonging. This class was my daily oasis, where I could communicate freely without fearing being mocked. The ESOL class was a melting pot of students from different backgrounds with

the same issue of language barrier. I met other Haitian students here, and for the first time since arriving in America, I felt a genuine connection. I also had the fortune that my class schedule mirrored that of my friend, Noële, whom I had met earlier in high school. Together, we navigated other classes, lending each other support and courage. Looking back, I can't help but wish that my middle school had offered an ESOL program exactly like this. It would have made those years less daunting. I met other immigrant kids like myself who had grown up under strict religious guidelines in the United States. Suddenly, I no longer felt as if I was the oddball in the room. All I needed to do was find my niche.

    As I ventured deeper into my college education, majoring in biology as per the well-laid plans of my parents, a startling realization dawned upon me. This path wasn't my calling; it was their dream for me. In Haitian culture, career options are often narrowly defined as the esteemed careers of a nurse, doctor, or lawyer. Venturing outside these traditional choices is seen as stepping off the path to success. My mother had her heart set on me becoming a doctor. As a true mama's girl, I naturally wanted to make her proud. But as I delved into my biology studies, it became increasingly clear that this was a square peg in a round hole situation. I wasn't the top student in my class; I hovered around the B-C average mark, getting by but never excelling. Biology, however, was a different beast altogether. I remember sitting in that first class, feeling utterly lost, the concepts flying over my head. The dread of bringing home a failing grade was real, and it pushed me to make a decision. I changed my major without telling my parents. Instead, I earned a surgical technician degree.

    As I scrubbed into the Operation Rooms during my clinical, I realized a few critical things. While I found the work doable, there was no passion in it for me. The attitude of some doctors who treated techs poorly didn't sit well with me. Moreover, being in an environment surrounded by illness and suffering all day was disheartening. I knew I wanted to help people, but in a different way – not when they were already at their most vulnerable in a hospital bed.

College was like trying to find my way through a maze with no clear exit. I must have switched my major twice, thinking I'd found my path, only to hit another dead end. I had a surgical technician degree, but it was more a piece of paper than a gateway to a career I was passionate about. Then, I was tantalizingly close to completing a women's studies degree. I was just one class away when the realization hit me like a cold splash of water. What would I do with this degree? The decision to abandon my women's studies degree was surprisingly easy, driven by practical concerns and a deep-seated realization that it wasn't the right fit for me. I remember sitting across from a guidance counselor, hoping for clarity, a roadmap to a career that would use this degree.

Instead of answers, I found myself drowning in more questions. The counselor, with all good intentions, asked me what I was truly passionate about. That conversation was a turning point when I knew my foray into healthcare was officially over. I worked part-time as a sterile processing technician, but healthcare wasn't where my heart was. That's when the idea of a career in national security sparked a light in me. It dawned on me that I could be part of something bigger, a field where I could contribute to preventing harm rather than just treating it. The thought of being involved in protecting people, or stopping danger before it happened, was exhilarating.

Choosing national security as my vocation was like

finding a missing puzzle piece. It aligned with my desire to help and protect but in a proactive rather than reactive manner. The excitement of this new direction was a feeling I had never experienced with biology. It felt right like this was where I was meant to be. Of course, I could not easily share this shift in my career path with my parents. The fear of disappointing them, particularly my mother, weighed heavily on me. In our Haitian culture, deviating from the expected path is not just a personal choice; it's seen as turning your back on your family's hopes and dreams. The pressure to conform to their expectations was immense. But as I grew more confident in my new path, I knew I had to face them eventually. I was prepared for their disappointment, confusion, and maybe even anger. It was a tough pill to swallow, realizing that I might be letting down the two people who had sacrificed so much for me in chasing my dreams.

> "The excitement of this new direction was a feeling I had never experienced with biology. It felt right, like this was where I was meant to be."

Despite the dooming feeling of letting down my parents, it was overshadowed by my current life's revelation of my true passion and mustering the courage to pursue it. It taught me the assurance and importance of heeding my inner voice and the strength it takes to forge one's path. In choosing national security, I wasn't just picking a major; I was charting a new course for my life that was distinctly mine and not a reflection of someone else's dreams.

The next decision I made a decision finally set me on a definitive course. I joined the military. I spent four years on active duty and another four in the Army Reserve. In the disciplined routines and the spirit of service in the military, I found a sense of purpose. Serving and protecting resonated with me deeply. Inspired by my time in the military, I decided to embark on a degree in criminal justice. This time, it was different. I wasn't just going through the motions; I was genuinely interested in what I was learning. The core classes captivated me, and for once, I wasn't struggling to keep up or question my choices. There was a natural alignment between the course material and my interests, a harmony I hadn't found in my previous academic pursuits.

As I delved deeper into criminal justice, the excitement grew. I wasn't just acquiring knowledge but building a vision for my future. I wasn't entirely sure which agency I would join after graduating, but I was certain in my heart that I was in the right field. The subjects of law enforcement, criminology, and justice weren't just academic topics; they were the building blocks of a career where I could make a difference and protect and serve in a capacity that aligned with my values and experiences.

Completing my Bachelor of Science in Criminal Justice was more than just an academic milestone; it was the culmination of a long, winding journey. It was a series of trials and errors coming to an end. The process of elimination that led to a patient, slow resolution of fulfillment in my beginning journey of purpose in my career life! It taught me that it's okay not to have all the answers right away. I had to go through several wrong turns to find the right path. My journey through college, the military, and finally through criminal justice was finding where I belonged and discovering a career that excited me, challenged me, and aligned with my desire to serve and protect.

Chapter 5: A world beyond my Parents

For the first time, I was truly alone, miles away from the familiar comforts and constraints of my Haitian upbringing. The freedom was liberating yet intimidating, a double-edged sword that cut deep into my being. The things that look pretty compelling aren't that amusing once you get the entire view of the situation.

In my parents' home, life was structured with clear expectations and boundaries defined by our Haitian culture. Living in a world without those boundaries was liberating. The ability to think and act for myself, without fear of judgment or reprimand, opened up a new world of possibilities and experiences I never thought possible. Leaving the strict environment was like stepping into a void filled with excitement for the new life ahead and simultaneously guilt for abandoning the only world I knew. Being away from my parents also meant leaving my younger siblings behind. I couldn't shake off the guilt that came with this decision. I was torn between the relief of escaping a household that felt increasingly suffocating and the worry for my siblings who remained in that environment. These were the things that I didn't give much thought to before taking the step, but it did impact me after the move.

Every step I took towards my independence was weighed down by the thought of them, still under the watchful eyes of our parents, living a life I had desperately wanted to change. Though my parents loved me, they did not respect or approve of my decision to move out. Thus, my siblings were not allowed to visit me, even though my apartment was 20 minutes away. Our relationship was complex, with deep affection entwined with unyielding expectations. In their eyes, I was still the child who needed guidance, not an adult.

The feelings of loving my parents yet yearning for their respect and understanding of my choices became a constant inner dialogue. I longed for their approval, for them to see me as an individual with my dreams and aspirations. **I wanted them to see I still had value and love for them, even if I didn't follow their predetermined path. There was another way that I was following that would still yield much fruit.**

The emotions were raw and real. The fear of the unknown, the excitement of new possibilities, and the bittersweet realization that in pursuing my dreams, I was also stepping away from the life I once knew. On both spectrums, there was that creeping sense of loneliness. In Haitian culture, the idea of a child, especially a daughter, leaving home before marriage is almost unheard of. It's like breaking an unwritten rule, a deviation from a path well-trodden by generations. So, when I decided to take that step, it was met with more than just surprise; it was met with outright disapproval. My parents couldn't wrap their heads around my decision. From their perspective, my moving out was not just unconventional; it was a direct challenge to the values they had held dear all their lives.

The words exchanged in those heated moments were sharp, cutting deep.

They said things that made me vow never to return or set foot again in the family home. Little did I know that in just three months, I would find myself in a much more challenging situation, alone and without the family support I so desperately needed.

As I grew older, the disagreements with my father became constant. We were like two rams, continually butting heads, each standing firm on our beliefs and decisions. My mom, always caught in the middle, was torn apart by these conflicts. I could see the pain in her eyes, the struggle of being pulled in two directions – between her husband and her daughter. Watching her crumble under this pressure was heartbreaking, feeling like she had to choose sides. I thought leaving would make things easier for everyone. In my mind, removing myself from the equation was the best solution. I believed it would ease the tension, give my mom some peace, and maybe, just maybe, give my dad some time to see things from my perspective. Me moving out meant that my parents would no longer be a source of support. The relationship with my siblings was strained; they were too young and still under the influence of our parents. They couldn't reach out to me without our parents knowing, making them collateral damage. Yet, in the midst of all this, there was a part of me that held onto hope. Hope that bridges could be mended one day and that misunderstandings would be cleared. Despite our differences, I clung to the belief that the family bond could withstand even the most harrowing trials.

Moving out on my own was already a leap into the unknown. I had to stand on my own two feet for the first time. Sensing my apprehension, my boyfriend, Stephen, stayed with me for a while, providing emotional support and a sense of security. His presence was comforting, and for a brief period, I felt less isolated. A couple of months after Stephen's departure, the signs became impossible to ignore. I missed my period; I was gaining weight, but pregnancy was the last thing on my mind. I attributed the weight gain to the stress of adapting to my new environment. Three months into my journey of independence, life turned upside down for me, and it was something that I wasn't prepared for.

I discovered I was indeed pregnant. The news hit me like a ton of bricks, not just because of the pregnancy itself but because I felt utterly alone in dealing with it. At a time when I was still trying to find my footing in this new, independent life, suddenly, I was facing a future as a single, pregnant woman with no familial support to lean on. The reality of my situation was like a haunting. I could hear the words of my father as a teenager. Pregnancy was the worst thing and yet the most feared thing that could happen. Yet here I was. Feeling utterly overwhelmed, unsure of how to navigate the path ahead, and scared. After all, no one had prepared me for the harsh realities of adult life – the bills, the responsibilities, the way friends seemed to vanish when you needed them most.

> My mother had warned me, "You just want to leave here and get pregnant like I did."

Here I was, a young woman trying to forge her path, now facing an unplanned pregnancy with little to no support system. My pregnancy felt like a bitter echo of history. My mother had warned me, "You just want to leave here and get pregnant like I did." Her words stuck with me, a haunting reminder of how parents can unwittingly shape their children's futures with their words. The power of the tongue, I realized, was not to be underestimated. It was a lesson in how the fears and expectations of parents can be imposed upon their children, sometimes turning into self-fulfilling prophecies. It was beyond me how this happened.

During that hectic period, every day felt like running a marathon with no finish line. Juggling two jobs and college courses, all while grappling with the reality of my pregnancy, was depleting me. There were moments, lots of them when I felt utterly swamped. Mornings were the most challenging – waking up to the same grind, the weight of my secret pregnancy adding to the fatigue. I'd lie there for a few extra minutes, gathering the willpower to get up and face the world. Those few minutes were my brief respite, a tiny window of calm before plunging into the day's chaos. The fact that I couldn't turn to my family for support added a layer of emotional complexity to the mix. Despite everything, I missed the comfort of leaning on someone, especially my mom. But our relationship hit rock bottom after I moved out. They had their stance, and I had mine, leaving a gulf between us filled with unspoken words and unsentimental feelings.

Keeping my pregnancy a secret meant withdrawing from any social circles I had. I watched from the sidelines, often with envy, as my classmates chatted about plans and parties. Once again, that world seemed so distant, like a TV show I used to watch but could no longer relate to. I'd often think about my future, about the life growing inside me. It was scary, yet there was a certain thrill in facing the unknown and proving to myself that I could do this. Each night, as I collapsed into bed, exhausted to the bone, there was a slight sense of accomplishment. I had made it through another day.

Looking back, I realize those months shaped me in ways I hadn't anticipated. They taught me the art of finding strength in vulnerability. I learned that what I thought were my limits were obliterated! I was fueled not by despair but by the power of hope. It kept me going even when the odds seemed stacked against me. Life had become gritty. I was experiencing a real-life lesson but faced it head-on with all its messiness and uncertainties. The sense of isolation was real, eating me up on the inside, wrapping around me like a thick fog. Each day, I trudged through, working two jobs, attending college, and trying to keep my head above water financially and emotionally.

The challenges were relentless. I was living paycheck to paycheck, constantly worrying about money casting a long shadow over my days. The joy of independence quickly gave way to the harsh reality of financial struggles. I had managed to save just enough to cover the initial costs of my apartment, but beyond that, there was nothing – no safety net, no cushion to fall back on. In those moments of despair, I often found myself questioning my decisions. The freedom I had sought in moving out seemed like a distant memory, replaced by the stark reality of my current situation.

But after all, I was the eldest of daughters, raised to be the strongest of all. So, there was a part of me that refused to give up. It was this refusal to be beaten down that kept me going. I had chosen to carve out my path and was determined to see it through, no matter how hard it got. I clung to the hope that things would get better and that I would find a way. During those dark times, my relationship with faith took a significant turn.

I needed that source back. Remember, when I finally got the freedom to live independently, one of the first things I did was step away from the church. I stopped attending services, praying, and even thinking about God. This detachment from my religious upbringing left a void during my pregnancy. In those moments of isolation and hardship, when I struggled to make ends meet and grappled with the reality of being pregnant and alone, I felt the absence of that spiritual anchor even greater than my family's lack of presence. The support system that only faith can provide was missing, and I couldn't help but feel all the more alone. It's strange how the absence of something you once considered a burden suddenly feels like a loss. Growing up, being part of the church community was just a natural part of life. But now, living on my own, I've come to truly appreciate how much that community, the faith, and the fellowship are essential.

Looking back, I can see how this shift in my spiritual life impacted me. It was more than just missing out on church services; it was about losing a source of comfort, guidance, and strength that I didn't even realize I depended on until it was gone. I often reflected on my upbringing, the values instilled in me, and how they clashed with the life I was leading. I was caught in a tug-of-war between the lessons from my past and my present realities, trying to find a balance and a sense of peace amid the chaos.

When my father and my mother forsake me, then the Lord will take me up.

PSALM 27:10 (KJV)

Chapter 6:

Finding Me....

By now, if you have had any resonance with my story you can see how many of us, immigrant's children, need community all the more after moving to the United States. I overcame the isolation, the lower self-esteem, and even mental challenges but the dialogue of discovering Mirline Dort was so much bigger than the story of a immigrant girl trying to navigate her way.

The father I grew up with was not my biological father. The story of my mother's escape with me in her arms, a mere infant from the life of isolation and control she faced with my biological father, Raynaud, always felt surreal. It was like listening to a dramatic tale, but it was real, and so was my story. I grew up oblivious to the sacrifice and the choice she had to make - to bring me into a new life, away from a father who wanted to erase my existence if I wasn't under his control.

My mother's recollection of those days painted a picture of a woman desperate for freedom, not just for herself but for her baby girl. She spoke of the nights she felt like a prisoner, unable to connect with the world outside, her every move monitored. The night she ran away with me, she chose a path that would change our lives forever. In doing so, she defied a man who couldn't fathom the idea of not having complete control.

Meeting my biological father after all these years was a confrontation with a past I had never known. The man before me was a stranger, yet he was a part of me. I was a bundle of nerves when I met my biological father at 28. I had been looking forward to that moment ever since I learned about him, but nothing truly prepares you for something like this. It was like stepping into a parallel universe where I had a different life and story. The anxiety had my heart racing with every step I took towards him. The meeting was short, filled with awkward silences and hesitant conversations. It was a bittersweet experience, a closure to a chapter of my life that had always been shrouded in mystery.

In contrast, connecting with my siblings was an unexpected joy. They were like strangers who felt like family. Their warmth and acceptance were overwhelming, filling in gaps in my heart I didn't even realize existed. It was incredible to discover these bonds that were always there, just waiting to be unearthed. They were the silver lining in this complex emotional journey. Their acceptance and eagerness to connect were heartwarming. Each story they shared, every memory they recounted, made me feel like I was piecing together parts of my life that I didn't even know were missing.

I was finding new family connections and rediscovering parts of myself. I was then acutely aware of a unique fact about my family: out of all my siblings, I was the only one who didn't grow up with our father. He raised his 14 other children, my older siblings, and there I was, the odd one out, the only child who didn't get to be with him. This detail of my life always hung in the background, a constant reminder of a connection I missed.

For the longest time, I coped with this by telling myself that it was his loss, not mine. It was easier to think that way, to believe that his absence was his mistake, a choice he would regret. This thought became a shield, protecting me from the hurt and confusion of why he wasn't a part of my life. Bless her heart; my mom brought up the topic occasionally. She would ask if I wanted to meet him, perhaps hoping to mend that broken bond. But every time she asked, my response was a firm no. I wasn't ready, or maybe I was too scared to face the flood of emotions that such a meeting would undoubtedly bring. The idea of my biological father raising all my siblings except me was a puzzle I couldn't solve. These questions would swirl in my mind, but deep down, I hesitated to find the answers. There was a part of me that feared what those answers might reveal.

> 'Why was I the exception? Was it something about me, or were the circumstances beyond my control?

Despite these feelings, there was also a sense of curiosity, a part of me that wondered what life would have been like if I had grown up with him and my siblings. Would I be a different person? Would I understand myself better? These questions had no answers, just speculations and what-ifs. As I grew older, my perspective on the situation gradually shifted. I began to see it less as a personal loss and more as a part of my life that shaped me in ways I didn't realize. Not growing up with my father and siblings gave me a different view of family and relationships. It taught me the value of the connections we choose to make and those we prefer to maintain.

So, while I didn't have the conventional upbringing with my biological father and siblings, I had something else – a life that was mine to shape, a journey of discovery that was unique to me. In my mid-20s, a sudden curiosity took hold of me – a desire to connect with a part of my life that had always been a mystery. For years, my biological father was just a shadowy figure in the background of my story, someone I had convinced myself didn't matter. But as I grew older, my feelings began to shift. It wasn't so much about him anymore but about the siblings I had never known. After constantly being the eldest of four, the idea of having older brothers and sisters sparked an intrigue that I couldn't shake off.

I decided it was time to seek out my father. It was more about piecing together the missing parts of my past than a longing for a relationship with him. My mom, ever supportive, agreed to join me on this quest. We planned a trip to Haiti, to the neighborhood where he used to live, hoping to find some clue, some lead that would bring me closer to the family I never knew. Landing in Haiti felt like stepping into a chapter of my life that had remained unopened. Everything was imbued with nostalgia and mystery: the streets, the sounds, the air. My mother and I made our way to his old neighborhood, our hearts a mix of anticipation and apprehension. Our search hit a dead-end almost as soon as it began. The neighbors we spoke to remembered him, but their stories all ended with the same conclusion – he had left for the U.S. long ago. Where in the U.S., they couldn't say. It was a revelation that both surprised and disappointed me. Here I was, where my father once lived, yet he felt more elusive than ever.

Despite the dead-end search for my biological father, being in Haiti stirred something in me. It connected me to my roots, to a part of my heritage that I had only ever known through stories. Walking the streets he once walked, talking to people who once knew him brought me closer to a past I had only ever imagined. My curiosity increased. The idea of having older siblings out there somewhere continued to fascinate me. I wondered about their lives and stories and whether they ever thought about the sister they hadn't met.

Did they know about me?

Returning from Haiti, I was no closer to finding my father

or siblings, but the trip wasn't in vain. It sparked a deeper understanding of my heritage and a renewed curiosity about my family's history. My search for my father and any trace of him had turned into something of a routine. Night shifts at my security job in Atlanta gave me plenty of time to think and often scour the internet for any information. Spokeo, Google, social media – you name it, I'd tried it. But every search ended in a dead-end, leaving me with more questions than answers.

Then, on a seemingly ordinary night in July 2015, everything changed. I was at work, the clock edging towards 1 a.m., boredom weighing heavily on me. To pass the time, I logged into Facebook and, on a whim, reached out to a group I had joined. Everyone in the group shared my last name, a quirky little community that I thought was cool. That night, out of sheer boredom, I posted a message in the group, asking if anyone knew a person with my father's full name. I didn't think much of it after that. It was just another shot in the dark, something to break the monotony of my shift. I closed Facebook and returned to work, the message slipping from my mind.

A couple of days later, I received two messages that turned my world upside down. They were from two women who, as it turned out, were my sisters. I remember staring at my phone screen, disbelief and excitement mingling in a strange cocktail of emotions. One of my sisters, Ava, wanted my number right away. She had follow-up questions about the story I'd shared, and I found myself recounting the little I knew about our father. We agreed she would call me back. In the meantime, I chatted with my other sister, who, to my utter shock, sent me a current picture of our father. I forwarded the picture to my mom, my heart pounding with anticipation. Her response was almost immediate – a phone call filled with surprise and recognition. "Where did you find him?" she asked, her voice a mix of astonishment and something else I couldn't quite place.

"Is that him?" I asked her, needing confirmation.

> Her answer was a simple yet profound, "That's him."

In that moment, everything became real. The years of wondering, the idle searches, and the questions that lingered in mind all culminated in this surreal revelation. Here I was, 28 years old, post-military life, working on my undergrad degree, and suddenly, I had a connection to a part of my life that had always felt like a missing puzzle piece. That night, the conversation with my sisters opened a new chapter in my life. It was a mix of emotions – excitement at getting to know them, apprehension about what this meant for my understanding of my family, and a deep curiosity about the father I never knew. It felt like I was standing at the threshold of a new world, one where the past and present were about to intertwine in ways I had never imagined. I was bridging the gaps in my personal history, about understanding where I came from, and about the intricate web of relationships that had shaped my life from afar.

Following my Facebook post led me to an impromptu meeting that very night. My sister was eager to meet me after confirming that we were related. While exciting, her invitation sparked a whirlwind of anxieties.

"Tonight?", I found myself asking, a mix of excitement and disbelief in my voice. She lived only an hour away, and suddenly, everything felt overwhelmingly real. There I was, a single woman, alone at home, contemplating meeting a sister I had just discovered on social media. It felt like something straight out of a movie – surreal and slightly unnerving. Part of me was cautious, reminding myself this was not a typical situation. But another part of me felt an instant connection to this newfound sibling and was filled with eager anticipation. Ava arrived at my place that night, accompanied by my niece. As we talked, she confirmed that our father remembered my mother and me. That acknowledgment, albeit brief, was significant. It was a piece of the puzzle falling into place, confirming the stories I had grown up hearing.

A few weeks later, I was on a road trip to New York with Ava to meet our father and other siblings. The journey was a mix of emotions – curiosity, apprehension, and a sense of completing a journey that had started years ago. Meeting my father was an experience that I had mentally prepared for. I had penned down my thoughts and feelings as a way to clarify to myself why I was doing this. I knew where I stood. I had a dad who had raised me with love and care; I wasn't looking to replace him. My intention was clear. It wasn't about forming a bond with my biological father but connecting with my siblings. As for him, I wanted my biological father to see that I was doing well! Despite his absence, I had grown into a person who was happy and successful in her own right. I wanted him to know that I didn't harbor any expectations or desires for material things from him. In our interactions, it was evident that our father didn't have much to say to me. There was a distance, an unspoken acknowledgment of the years of separation and silence. Despite the initial awkwardness and the unspoken barriers, there was a silent understanding, an unexpressed acknowledgment of our shared bloodline.
I had walked into this part of my life without expectations, a decision that served me well. My father, shaped by the

staunch pride characteristic of many Haitian men, wasn't one to open up or offer explanations, especially not to his youngest child, whom he had not raised. I equally proud and stubborn, refused to prod for answers. Countless questions were swirling in my mind, a desire to understand, to know more about him, and by extension, about myself. Yet, my pride stood in the way. I believed I shouldn't have to ask; the answers should come to me, offered freely as a gesture of acknowledgment for my effort to find him.

    My siblings were a different story. They went out of their way to make me feel welcome, to weave me into the fabric of their lives as if I had always been there. Their efforts to distract me from the awkwardness with our father were touching, filling the gaps his silence left. Getting to know each of my siblings was like opening a series of windows into lives that had run parallel to mine yet never intersected. Each sibling had their own story, experiences with their father, and perspective on life. Our interactions included catching up on lost time and building new memories. My siblings didn't hold back in sharing their stories. Through their eyes, I saw different shades of our father, glimpses of a man I never knew. Their stories painted a more complex picture of him, which was intriguing and disheartening.

    My siblings and I would often meet, sometimes just for casual dinners or impromptu get-togethers. During these gatherings, we shared not just stories about our father but also our own life experiences. It was fascinating to see the similarities and differences among us. Some traits were unmistakably inherited, like a gesture or a way of laughing, that made me feel a sense of belonging I hadn't realized I was missing. The days following the initial meeting with my father and siblings turned into weeks, and the weeks soon stretched into months and years.

I found myself continuing to visit my father, a routine that became part of my life. As time went by my father's health began to decline, my perspective started to shift. Watching him grow frailer, a sense of compassion overshadowed my initial resentment and pride. Like everyone else's, it became clear that his life was a tapestry of choices and consequences. He was an older man who had lived a life full of complexities and, perhaps, regrets. Toward the end, I found myself forgiving him. It was not a grand gesture but a quiet acceptance in my heart. More than anything, I felt a profound sense of sadness for him.

Despite having fathered many children, he was essentially alone in his final days. He had not managed to keep close any of the women he had children with, and while my siblings and I were there for him, it was evident that he had no significant other, no 'person' to be by his side. His loneliness in those final moments was a reminder of the impact of one's actions over a lifetime. Despite our complicated relationship and the many unanswered questions, I felt a pang of empathy for this man who was my biological father. I felt like he missed out on being a part of my life and so much more.

This season of my life was called forgiveness. The complexities of human relationships showed me how pride can both protect and prevent us from more profound connections. Ultimately, it wasn't just about finding my father or getting to know my siblings. It was about learning to let go of pride, the power of forgiveness, and the human need for connection and understanding. The journey started with a search for answers and ended with a deeper understanding of life, relationships, and myself. Getting to spend time with my biological father before he passed away was a bittersweet experience. In hindsight, I wish I had been more upfront with him and asked all those tricky questions that swirled in my mind. Two years after his passing, I visited his gravesite. Seeing the myriad of emotions playing across my face, a friend asked me a seemingly simple question,

"How do you feel?"

    That question stumped me. The truth was, I hadn't fully processed his death yet. A part of me felt guilty, almost ashamed, for not being able to articulate my feelings. They seemed too complex, too tangled to put into words. At his funeral, I remember feeling a deep sadness, not so much for myself but for my siblings. Their grief was palpable, their loss profound. They had lost a father they had known all their lives, while I had lost a father I was beginning to understand. I observed their pain and tears, and while I shared in their sorrow, my grief differed. I mourned the lost opportunities, the unanswered questions, the what-ifs. I wished for more time, not just with him, but for the potential of our relationship.

    Meeting my siblings has been an entirely different experience. They were the missing puzzle pieces. Growing up as the oldest of four and suddenly finding out you're the youngest of fifteen is quite a twist. Talk about a shift in perspective! It's a fun fact I sometimes drop in conversations, watching people's reactions range from disbelief to amusement. It's a story that always surprises me, a unique aspect of my life that adds a bit of humor to my narrative. While I may have missed out on growing up with my biological father and siblings, the relationships I've built with them have added new dimensions to my life. They've filled the empty spaces of my heart that I didn't know were empty and provided answers to questions I didn't know I had.

One of the greatest joys of having other siblings is becoming an aunt, a title I hold close to my heart. Being an aunt allows me to connect with my nieces and nephews in a special way, and I get to see just how incredible they are as individuals. Since we're close in age, I have the unique opportunity to experience them from a different perspective. Our conversations are meaningful, and the trust they place in me is something I truly cherish. It's one of the most rewarding roles I've ever had, and I'm so grateful for the bond we share.

Having a relationship with my nieces and nephews gave me a different perspective, more than just being an older sibling. They talked to me in ways that allowed me to be nurturing and become a voice of reasoning and understanding, even when they didn't want to hear it from my sibling or their parent. Hindsight, what was to be revealed next, you will understand why these relationships were especially important to me.

In my journey of self-discovery, I've continually sought balance between understanding the pieces that shaped me—finding closure in knowing who my biological father was and gaining a bigger family structure to include more siblings and their children. Beyond the rocky start to independence, this healing was crucial in moving forward. I needed to find peace past what seemed like never-ending struggles and disappointments. What I uncovered next was undoubtedly the biggest trajectory shift in my life to truly finding myself. This wasn't so much about where I came from...but what came from me.

Chapter 7:
The Adoption Process

    Unknown to anyone, I was caught in a huge juggling act, trying to keep everything afloat and hiding my growing belly from those around me, especially my family. I was pregnant. However, due to the circumstances of my current life structure, my biggest focus was to maintain some semblance of normalcy as a 19-year-old teenager trying to start a new life. That, within itself, is nothing of the norm for a teenager. However, the resilience that was being birthed in me simultaneously at the same time was shaping my determination to not go back nor give up a chance to prove to myself that I could succeed past this season. Life seemed to speed up just as quickly as the notion of the pregnancy becoming a real fact that I could not deny, even to myself. I was hustling between two jobs and chipping away at my degree, all while carrying this big secret. While finding creative ways to hide my pregnancy, including wearing two girdles at times, it was tough feeling alone in the midst of it all. There were no shoulders to lean on or hands to grasp. I was alone, navigating this storm, keeping up appearances on the outside.

Despite the challenges, the mounting bills, and the struggle to put food on the table, I was unwavering in my decision to keep my unborn child. There were many moments where, after working both my full-time and part-time jobs, paying the bills, and filling up the gas tank, I was left with just $20 to last two weeks for groceries. You might wonder, "How could anyone survive on that?" But for me, it was a familiar reality. I learned how to stretch every dollar, making simple meals like spaghetti with hotdogs or white rice with chicken stew, using just a few ingredients like chicken drumsticks, a bag of rice, hotdogs, and tomato paste. With homemade seasonings, those meals sustained me for days. Even as my pregnancy progressed, this was my way of life, and the fear of being trapped in that cycle felt overwhelming.

After the internal denial that I was pregnant, the fact of the matter settled in, and I knew I needed to start receiving prenatal care. After my second appointment, the connection became real. I learned I was carrying a little girl, and from that moment on, I knew I loved her. While I was certain I wanted to keep her, I couldn't ignore the harsh truth. I was barely surviving myself, and I couldn't bring a child into that level of hardship. Asking my family for help wasn't an option. Our relationship was strained, and I was deeply afraid of the shame it would bring, not just to them but to the church as well. My parents were deacons in their church, and having a daughter with a baby out of wedlock was not ideal. I knew they would bear the consequences of my choices, and I didn't want them to be punished for my actions. In the end, I made the heart-wrenching decision to place my daughter for adoption—not because I didn't love her, but because I wanted her to have the life I couldn't provide. As a single woman with no financial resources and no family support, I had no means of meeting her needs.

Truth be told, adoption was a means to an end. I did not comprehend the depth of the choice, nor did I realize how painful it would be.

Then, the day came when I had to talk to my ex-boyfriend, Stephen, about the future of our little one. It wasn't easy to figure out how to even contact him after months of no communication. Our first conversation was tense—so much so that we had to hang up before it escalated further. I decided to cut to the chase and texted him, "I'm pregnant." Almost immediately, the phone rang. I had been dreading his response, bracing myself for anger, blame, or resistance. But what he said surprised me. I had been dreading the next response, yet it was surprisingly straightforward. His response caught me off guard. I had braced myself for the resistance. He asked, "How will you manage?" His question wasn't accusatory but rooted in concern.

I loosely outlined my thoughts, but I had made up my mind to choose placement via adoption. If there had been any pushback, I knew my path would have been much more complicated. Surprisingly, he didn't object. Instead, he quietly agreed with my decision. This support was unexpected but deeply appreciated, especially since his agreement to relinquish his parental rights was crucial to the adoption process.

The biggest hurdle of the process was having that conversation. The next step was making it a reality. I had no clue where to start, what steps to take, or how to navigate the legalities. During this time of uncertainty, Stephen proposed an idea that hadn't crossed my mind, which was having one of his family members adopt the baby. This suggestion was clutching at straws while drowning at sea. The thought brought some form of peace, a hopeful comfort amid my confusion surrounding it all.

The thought of her staying with the family meant I could ensure she was loved and cared for. It meant I would still be a part of her life, in some way, keeping that invisible thread between us intact. Everyone was on board, and we came together in a rare moment of unity and shared purpose. We all agreed this was the best way forward. It felt right, settling on a decision that kept her close, surrounded by family. This plan, while unconventional, offered peace amidst the storm of emotions and decisions that had defined this journey so far.

What seemed to be a light at the end of the tunnel moment came to a halt! I had imagined the moment—handing my baby girl to a family member I trusted, someone who could love and care for her better than I could've imagined. This perfect solution, which gave me a sense of peace in an otherwise turbulent time, vanished just like that. I was suddenly left holding a map with no clear destination! The plans had fallen through. With my hands being able to rest on the swell of my belly, deep into my pregnancy, and with time slipping away, I found myself without a plan, exhausted and overwhelmed. The weight of it all pressed down on me as I sat there, my heart heavy with the unexpected.

The ground beneath me seemed to shake even more. I was attempting to balance an internship, which was crucial for my graduation. However, dealing with the emotional rollercoaster of the adoption process had me running on empty. As if that wasn't enough, I was on the verge of losing my apartment. Now, financial struggles weren't new to me, but the timing couldn't have been worse. Amidst all this chaos, losing my home felt like the universe was piling on more than I could bear. My mind was racing with questions like,

"How does one even start an adoption?"
"Would it be an open or closed adoption?"
" How am I going to pay for these hospital bills?"

And the biggest question yet,
"How do I stop this eviction notice on my doorstep?"

In desperation and not knowing where else to turn, I turned to the internet for help. Searching for private adoption agencies became a nightly ritual, a search for a lifeline amid a storm. The bills were stacking up, a constant reminder of the precariousness of my situation. I didn't have any insurance, so every doctor's visit was a financial hit, and keeping the lights on was becoming increasingly difficult. Miraculously, just when I thought there was no resolution present, a kind-hearted Samaritan stepped in and lent me enough money to cover all the court fees that had been looming over me because of the lack of paying the rent. Their generosity saved me from the brink of losing my apartment, allowing me to hold onto the one stable part of my life amidst all the chaos. That victory, small but significant, gave me the space and relief I needed to continue my search for an adoption agency. This task was daunting as I reached out to various agencies until I found one that felt right. With each agency presenting new information, promises, and processes to sift through.

I had no time to waste. Thankfully, they were responsive, understanding, and most importantly, made me feel heard. When I got to the stage of finally setting up the appointment, it felt like a significant step forward. This was really happening! The ladies at that office saw my desperation and hardship, and they were kind enough to lend me an ear. They answered every question and scenario

I threw at them. They clarified the difference between a closed adoption and an open adoption. Then, they gave me options. It was the first time in weeks that I finally felt like I could breathe again. Deciding on an open adoption for my little girl was hard. I was scared, but more than anything, I was hopeful for the life this decision could give her.

    Amid financial woes and personal trials, I discovered an inner strength. Even when the path ahead was unclear, there was always a way through the fog. All I had to do was take one step at a time, putting one foot in front of the other. Even if all I could see was that step, I was going to be ok. Looking back on everything I've been through, it's pretty clear there was always some guiding force in my life. Even when I felt like I had turned away and was all caught up in my problems, I wasn't left to fend for myself. It's incredible to think about the moments when people just showed up for me, offering kindness and support when I least expected it but needed it the most. For example, this one teacher could have easily overlooked me as just another student struggling to stay awake in class. Instead, he saw someone needing a bit more attention and guidance.

    Opening up to him helped me get my grades back up and reminded me that people cared and that I wasn't as invisible as I felt. The biggest moment of help came from a family friend. They reached out right when things were looking pretty bleak for me. I was staring down an eviction notice, with nowhere to turn, and not ready to crawl back to a family I felt disconnected from. Hearing about my predicament, they didn't hesitate to offer the financial help I needed to keep my apartment. It was more than just the money; it was a lifeline, a gesture of genuine kindness. With their help, I talked to my landlord and honestly shared my situation. I needed grace. The understanding she showed me was another one of those unexpected blessings, giving me just enough time to get my finances in order and pay off what I owed. I had to take out private student loan from the school, which took some of the weight off my shoulders. Not only could I pay back the generous family friend, but I also cleared some of my other outstanding debts, including the utilities and rent, which gave me room to breathe. All these experiences, these acts of kindness from people who crossed my path, make me think it wasn't all just a coincidence. Looking at it now, I know there was a hand guiding me, placing these helpers in my life right when I needed them most. During a time when I was too stubborn to seek out help, it found me anyway. It was none other than God's hand, leading me that everything turned out so much in my favor. These things led me further onto the path of finding God and staying connected.

What I learned about God's favor and protection was that it is constant, unwavering, and unearned. He always showing up exactly as you need, even when you don't realize it or feel deserving. Even when we don't ask for His help—perhaps because we feel too broken, too far gone, or simply unworthy of His love—He covers us with protection, making a way where there seemed to be none. Even when it came to hitting the reset button after the plans fell through with the family member taking in my unborn daughter. The clock was ticking, and my pregnancy was progressing, but it was time to revisit the crucial task at hand, which was finding a loving home for my daughter.

As much as the option for her to be with Stephen's family was a desirable option for me, the confirmation that the family member had backed out wasn't a shock. Deep down, I'd prepared myself for this possibility. However, there was no time to dwell on Plan A's collapse; I was already knee-deep into Plan B. I'd love to paint a picture of a meticulous selection process where I weighed every option with the gravity it deserved. But the truth? I was still in survival mode. My decisions were driven more by necessity than by an idealized selection process. Choosing the family for my daughter wasn't about having all the answers or making the perfect decision. It was about learning how to trust. I had to trust the process of my life and that it was going to turn out for good. I had to trust that God was bringing me the right people to help guide me through it. Ultimately, the most resounding trust that began to shape my courage was to trust myself to make the best choice in a far from ideal situation. Out of all the things I could focus on, I had to become resolute in the fact that this was a decision made with love, hope, and a sincere wish for her future happiness and well-being despite how she was going to come into the world. She was destined to be here. It taught me about the strength found in vulnerability, the importance of seeking and accepting help, and the unbreakable bond of maternal love that guides even the most challenging decisions.

  Finally, I was presented with a stack of portfolios, each representing a potential future for her. It was an overwhelming moment, knowing that the decision I was about to make would shape the rest of her life. Each portfolio was a window into a different world, full of strangers who could become her family. I found myself looking for signs of kindness in their photos, reading their letters with a fine-tooth comb for sincerity, and evaluating their financial stability not out of materialism but out of a deep-seated desire for her to have the security I struggled to find. Selecting a family based on a few pages of information felt surreal, like trying to read the future in tea leaves. Yet, there was one portfolio that stood out. It wasn't just their smiling faces or the warmth that seemed to emanate from their words; the sense of genuine kindness permeated their profile. They spoke about their desire to provide a loving home, their understanding of the responsibility that comes with adoption, and their financial readiness to provide for her in every way possible.

I whispered a prayer for my little girl....

As I made my choice, my heart was heavy with the magnitude of the decision. I whispered a prayer, asking for guidance, hoping that I was making the right choice for my little girl. It was a leap of faith, trusting strangers with the most precious part of my life, based on a feeling that they were the right ones. Choosing her future family was a process that was a mix of fear, hope, and a profound sense of responsibility. I wanted more than anything for her to grow up in a home filled with love, laughter, and opportunities I could only dream of providing. It was about letting go, trusting that these people I had never met could give her the life she deserved. In the days that followed, I often second-guessed my decision, wondering if I had read the signs correctly. But every time I revisited their portfolio, I felt a sense of peace and reassurance that this was the right choice.

The lawyer asked me a deep question. What did I want my daughter to know about her adoption? My heart knew the answer instantly. I

> " If she ever asked...what did I want my daughter to know about why she was adopted? "

needed her to understand that this decision was made out of love. I chose adoption, not because I didn't want her, but because I wanted more for her than I could provide. Every moment we shared during the pregnancy was precious, and the decision to let her go was tough. Accepting that this was the right decision took a lot of soul-searching and therapy. It was a harsh realization but made from a place of love. Choosing to go through the placement process was without a doubt, the hardest and most selfless act of love I could offer. It wasn't a decision I made lightly, and it certainly wasn't because I didn't love her—quite the opposite. It was because I loved her so deeply that I had to think beyond my own desires and dreams, beyond my own pain, and focus on what was best for her life.

I knew I wasn't in a place to give her the stability and future she deserved, and that realization broke my heart. But my love for her was so great that I was willing to endure the sacrifice so she could have something better. I wasn't just giving her up—I was giving her the chance to live a life filled with the kind of love, support, and opportunities I couldn't provide for her right now.

The thought of not being the one to hold her, to watch her grow, to be a part of her everyday life—it hurt more than I could express. But I've come to understand that love isn't always about holding on; sometimes, it's about letting go when that's what's best for the one you care about. Even though I wasn't going to be the one raising her, my love for her was always going to be with her. Before finalizing the adoption, I had a moment with the adoptive parents to emphasize how important it was for me to stay updated about her. The thought of not knowing anything about her life was unbearable. Reflecting on the placement experience, it was clear that God's guiding presence throughout this challenging season kept me. Every tough decision, moment of doubt, and step forward was surrounded by what the Bible refers to as peace that surpasses all understanding. Making a choice for adoption, finding peace with this decision, and entrusting another family with my daughter's care weren't steps I took entirely on my own.

God's hand was a quiet, steady presence in my life, even in the moments when the world felt like it was unraveling and darkness surrounded me. The guidance wasn't loud, but it was obvious because it created peace in my heart. His peace, unlike anything we could create on our own, has the power to settle our racing minds and anxious hearts. It's the kind of peace that doesn't make sense, given the chaos we might be facing, yet it comes, wrapping around us like a comforting blanket. When we are overwhelmed and uncertain, His hand gently guides us, reminding us that we are never alone. The whispers of hope, in the moments of unexpected strength, and the small victories remind me that we are held in His care. His saving grace stepped in, offering forgiveness, renewal, and the chance to begin again. It all pointed to a larger plan unfolding.

As things began to shift, the tide was also turning, and I began to notice my relationship with my family slowly being restored. It was a blessing I hadn't expected but very much so needed. I owe much of it to my younger siblings, who played peacemakers, convincing my parents to open their doors to me again, even just for visits. Their efforts created room for small reunions that were bittersweet, filled with unspoken words and tentative steps toward understanding. The familiar warmth I had missed more than I realized, starting a sense of healing I needed. I do believe in our physical time together; my mother was able to pick up on the things that I wasn't saying, but she knew how to respond. She would send me home with food, subtly easing one of the many burdens I carried. This gesture was a lifeline during a time when every bit of help mattered. I would have never imagined life would bring me to this place. But everything happens for a reason. What would appear to be the most chaotic time of my life was the inner workings of the beginning of reconciliation, purpose being born, resilience being perfected through me, and an undeniable undisputed love from God that I didn't need to question more than I just needed to trust.

And I would need that with what was about to happen next. During my seventh month, I had what I thought would be another normal checkup appointment with my obstetrician. But that day took an unexpected turn. After the ultrasound, the doctor seemed concerned and began to probe about my well-being. I responded but I was confused about this random line of questioning because everything felt the same to me. The silence that followed, with the doctor stepping out momentarily, only deepened my unease. When he returned, his words hit me like a freight train.

"She needs to be born today."

I was taken aback and bombarded with thoughts of unreadiness and denial. "What do you mean today?" I questioned, my mind racing through the reasons this couldn't happen. The doctor's words echoed in my head, but it was like my mind couldn't quite process them. Induced labor. Seven months. I wasn't ready—I thought I had more time. I'd just made the hardest decision of my life about adoption, finally settled on a family, and now everything was unraveling faster than I could keep up with. My heart pounded, and I felt a strange mix of panic and disbelief. How could this be happening so soon?

My pregnancy was still a secret from my work and parents! I had plans, obligations, and an internship that required my presence. And the thought of having a C-section terrified me, given that my family was still in the dark about my situation. The doctor tried to calm my spiraling thoughts, explaining that we'd try inducing labor first, reserving a C-section as a last resort. But what shook me to my core was learning that my daughter hadn't grown in the past few visits. Panic and guilt overwhelmed me as I couldn't help but think about the girdles I'd been wearing to hide my pregnancy.

"*Had I inadvertently harmed her?*" I was desperate for answers, fearing the worst that my actions had stunted her growth. The doctor assured me it wasn't my fault, yet no clear explanation was provided, leaving me with a lingering sense of self-blame and a multitude of unanswered questions. That day's events are etched in my memory and evoke the feelings I had as if it were just yesterday. Even now, writing about it brings back the flood of emotions I felt. A rush of fear washed over me, then the overwhelming guilt that perhaps my choices had endangered my daughter. Despite the doctor's reassurances, I've struggled to forgive myself, to shake off the shame that shadows my memories of that critical moment. There was no time to think, no space to breathe and process this moment. Everything was about to come crashing into my reality, and all I could do was brace myself for the impact.

When it suddenly became time to welcome my daughter into the world, I had to let the adoption agency know right away. The adoptive parents quickly came to the hospital, and the baby's father arrived the next day. Despite not being alone, I felt incredibly isolated, as if I were on the outside looking in on a significant moment in my life. I was a part of something that was happening to me but did not belong to me.

After I returned home from the hospital, I was so empty and heartbroken that I wept bitterly, and I tried repeatedly to call the agency to let them know I had changed my mind and I wanted my baby back, but each time, I was overcome with my love for her and her well-being. After all, I was sitting in my current circumstances with nothing. I had not purchased any baby food or clothing, nor did I have any means to do so.

Journal entry a month after I gave birth.....:

"It's been a month and 10-days since I gave birth to my baby girl and it's really hard, I miss her like crazy today in particular. I find myself wondering if I made the right decision? Is she happy? I don't know, my emotions are just all over the place. I just really miss her and wish that I could see her and hold her in my arms and tell her how much I love her and how sorry I am....."

> "And we know that all things work together for good to them that love God, to them who are the called according to his purpose."
> Romans 8:28 KJV

Chapter 8:
I Volunteered

Stepping into military life was like diving into a sea I'd never swum before—challenging yet thrilling. I can't recall when joining the military struck me, but it was perfect timing. Coping with what felt like a loss with the adoption of my daughter was difficult, so the military gave me a sense of purpose while suppressing my feelings.

This wasn't just about wearing a uniform; it was about embracing a new identity, one where the sense of duty intertwined with every aspect of my life. I quickly learned that in this world, actions didn't just speak; they roared. Despite the structured days and the rigid routines, there was something comforting about knowing exactly where I stood and what was expected of me. This was a world of difference compared to the uncertainty that had hampered me before. Yet, beneath this newfound stability, my thoughts often drifted to my daughter. Though not physical, her presence still continually guided my decisions and shaped my military experiences. I think failure was not an option because I had done something harder. The adoption could not be in vain. So, I always gave everything I did my all.

There were no half-hearted approaches here! Being in the military was the start of something incredible that shifted my life experiences. One of the best parts of it all was the camaraderie among my battle buddies. We became a family, understanding that we were part of something larger than ourselves. The sense of unity and striving toward a common goal was incredibly grounding. Every day, it reminded me that I am part of a team, a family forged not by blood but by shared purpose and mutual respect.

In this environment, I could put the broken pieces back together. When I joined I was at my lowest point. I was heartbroken and stuck in a void left by leaving that hospital without my daughter. The military provided me with the space I needed to remove the mask I was wearing for my family. It taught me the value of resilience, pushing through when every muscle protested, and every bone ached. More than the physical trials, the mental and emotional hurdles tested me the most. Yet, with each challenge I overcame, I discovered pieces of myself that I didn't know were lost. My fellow soldiers became my confidants, my brothers and sisters in arms, sharing the joys and sorrows that colored our days. The friendships that emerged in the most unexpected places became lifelines amid the chaos. I found refuge in these relationships built on mutual struggle and understanding. Amidst the hardship and loneliness, they provided solace and laughter.

One of the most profound lessons I carried with me is the art of strategic planning—reconnaissance. It wasn't just a military tactic; it became a way of life. Assessing situations, gathering information, and making informed decisions became second nature. This approach was invaluable in navigating the complexities of military operations and dealing with everyday dilemmas. It taught me the importance of being prepared, of never going into a situation blind, and of always having a plan. The skills I honed, and the relationships I built became integral parts of who I am, shaping my outlook on life and my approach to the world. Reflecting on this chapter of my life, I see it as a period of transformation—a time when I was molded by the trials I faced, buoyed by the bonds of friendship, and inspired by a sense of duty that went beyond the uniform. Ultimately, the military was a crucible that shaped, challenged, and led me to a deeper understanding of myself and my place in the world. It was a journey of coming to terms with my past, embracing the present, and looking forward to the future with hope and determination.

 I was stationed at Fort Drum, NY, which transported me light years away from Florida's eternal summer. This place, often quipped as the military's "best-kept secret," felt more like an outpost on the edge of civilization. The journey there was a trek across a seemingly infinite moment of barrenness, a dramatic shift from the lively atmosphere back home. At Fort Drum, I encountered a realm of extreme weather I hadn't fathomed existed. Encountering blizzards that muffled the world in white, navigating roads glazed with treacherous black ice, and learning the essential use of a block heater to keep your car from turning into an ice cube were all novelties for me. This chilly northern existence was a stark awakening for someone reared under Florida's sun.

 There was one winter that reinforced the perils of icy roads sternly. Having just cleared my car payments, I found myself in a heart-stopping slide across the ice, destroying my vehicle. Miraculously, I walked away without a scratch, a testament to luck or perhaps a watchful guardian. That harrowing slide was my rude introduction to the dangers of winter driving and the unforgiving nature of ice. The leap from Florida's shores to Fort Drum's snowy solitude and eventually to the challenging landscapes of Afghanistan charted an unpredictable path through my life. Each environment enriched my narrative with its distinct hurdles, sculpting me into the person I am now.

Answering the call for deployment to Afghanistan stirred a complex brew of emotions. Volunteering for the deployment was propelled by an adrenaline rush mixed with a genuine desire to be there for my comrades, the battle buddies who had become my second family. The gravity of this commitment weighed heavily on me. I wasn't just signing up for an adventure; I was confronting the war of possibly not returning home. The impending deployment cast shadows over the days leading up to our departure. Each moment was tinged with a sobering clarity about the challenges and dangers ahead.

My spiritual connection, which had taken a backseat amid the demands of military life and the whirlwind of personal changes, suddenly reached the forefront of my thoughts. There, in the belly of the C-130, with the engines humming a relentless reminder of the journey we were about to undertake, I found myself reaching out to God in a way I hadn't in years. My tears, which flowed uncontrollably down my cheeks as the aircraft ascended, weren't born of fear; instead, they were manifestations of my deep understanding of my journey. It was a profound moment of surrender, recognizing that the journey ahead demanded more than physical and mental preparation.

I was dependent solely on God to help me....

This season required spiritual readiness. I could not take on this challenge alone, especially if I were to survive in the wilderness. The leap into the unknown, with only my training and a thread of hope that it would suffice, marked a pivotal turning point. My situation didn't fully dawn on me until the plane's door closed, sealing off the only semblance of safety and leaving us unfamiliar. Life in Afghanistan unfolded in a relentless sequence of missions, vigilance, and the perpetual push to stay alert. The elusive peace I longed for seemed always out of reach, overshadowed by the omnipresent threat of sudden chaos. I rediscovered my faith in this constant high alert amidst the unforgiving landscape. My relationship with God was rekindled in the solitude and vastness of a war-torn country, and it became my anchor. It offered a solace that I clung to in the darkest of times. This wasn't a convenience-driven faith but a deeply personal, necessary connection that offered an approximation of peace in an otherwise tumultuous existence.

The weekly Sunday services became more than just a religious routine; they were a lifeline, a rare pocket of tranquility and community amidst the chaos. Gathering with fellow soldiers to share in this act of faith provided a much-needed respite, a moment to recharge and find solace in the shared understanding that we were never truly alone. This journey was transformative, marked by the dichotomy of war and faith, fear and courage, solitude and camaraderie. Another season of total dependence on God. Through cold winter months and sandy summer days, I was never alone. He has seen me through it all.

Living through a deployment is to live a life punctuated by trials that push you to the brink, not just physically but emotionally and spiritually. It transcended the mere act of fulfilling a mission; it encapsulated the essence of shared human experience, which is the desire to connect and find a foundational grounding to withstand any adversity with community, braving the storm with a unified resolve to persevere. Each day was unfurled with its challenges, demanding more than tactical acumen or physical endurance. It was about navigating through an ever-evolving landscape of uncertainty, where decisions bore weighty consequences, and actions could ripple far beyond our immediate surroundings if we reacted hastily. Amid this ever-present lack of knowing what was going to happen from moment to moment, the bond with my battle buddies became the beacon of stability. We were more than just a unit; we were a family, leaning on each other for tactical support and the emotional fortitude to greet each new day. This journey forced me to stare down my fears, reassess my convictions, and draw upon the combined strength of faith. A spiritual renaissance also marked this era. Re-engaging with my faith and immersing myself in the church community, I slowly began being pieced back together. This spiritual renewal, coupled with the geographical and emotional distance from my family, provided a sanctuary from the pain, allowing me to navigate daily life without the omnipresent shadow of my previous choices.

 Transitioning to a life where financial stability became my new norm was refreshing and surreal. No longer caught in the relentless cycle of living paycheck to paycheck, I found myself with the means to not just dream about a better future but actively pursue it. By shouldering the cost of my education, the military laid down a path for personal advancement I had hardly dared to envision. This newfound security allowed me to extend a helping hand back home, flipping the script and bringing a sense of fulfillment I hadn't expected.

 In the background a comforting progression was that

the connection with my daughter remained consistent. As promised, her adoptive parents provided updates. The precious moments I had the opportunity to spent with her during my scheduled breaks sketched a picture of the life we might have shared. Over time, the heartache that used to cloud the end of every visit dissipated, giving way to an appreciation for her happiness and well-being. Observing her flourish, even from a distance, nurtured a budding belief in the potential for my healing, fostering hope that witnessing familial bonds wouldn't always stir the cauldron of guilt and grief within me.

However, this facade of operating in total healing belied a deeper avoidance. The chasm between my pain and my everyday existence wasn't truly bridged; I had merely learned to sidestep the gap. My adeptness at relegating heartache to the background, at ignoring the simmering questions and emotions, wasn't resolution—it was evasion. With its structured demands and relentless pace, the military lifestyle conveniently masked this evasion. Wrapped up in the cocoon of orders and responsibilities, I found little space for introspection to grapple with my lingering sorrow.

But for what I could bring to immediate resolve was that life had finally begun to feel like it was balancing out, bringing a sense of peace I hadn't known in years. I found stability in areas that once felt impossible to attain—financial security, the sense of accepting community from fellow soldiers, the space I needed between myself and family, and the constant reminders of a difficult past as a head start of doing life on my own. This uniform and the principles of life I was learning and applying simultaneously gave me a sense of control over my life. I felt like I was finally moving forward.

Just as things began to equalize, a new and unexpected

challenge emerged, slowly overshadowing the sense of stability I was working hard to achieve. My health, once a source of strength, started to decline. What began as small, occasional discomfort soon turned into a relentless, ever-present pain, shifting the vitality I had always relied on. It wasn't just physical—it shook my confidence and began to cloud the very purpose I had rediscovered in the military. The pain became a constant reminder that life, no matter how stable it seemed, could shift in an unpredictable moment. A back injury was merely the prelude to a cascade of health issues that upended my previously unblemished medical record. Seasonal allergies transformed from a minor nuisance into a significant ordeal, ensuring my frequent presence in medical facilities. This shift from an epitome of health to battling chronic conditions was jarring. The military's one-size-fits-all remedy of ibuprofen and muscle relaxers was inadequate to respond to a complex problem. Persistent headaches became a grim reality, an unseen struggle that paralleled my commitment to duty.

    This reality, where duty perennially overshadowed personal well-being underscored a harsh truth: the military ethos of endurance often meant neglecting one's health. While symbolic of military resilience, this relentless push sometimes crossed into the realm of personal detriment. The journey from vibrant health to grappling with constant physical challenges was a bitter pill to swallow. Reflecting on the lively, healthy person I was when I first donned the uniform, the reality I now faced was a reminder of the sacrifices in service. Yet, though painful, the lessons drawn from these sacrifices have imparted wisdom that continued to shape my path. Facing the reality that my dedicated service might have left indelible marks, not just on my psyche but also on my body, stirred a tumult of feelings within me. The realization that the very essence of my patriotism and the vigor with which I served possibly was the root of my then current physical and mental strife was a complex notion to grasp. It's a paradox that intertwines pride with a tinge of uncanny regret, knowing that the uniform I wore with such honor would be the catalyst for my ailments.

    Despite the toll it took, the trials I faced in service helped me discover many unearthed traits and strengths within me that might have remained dormant. Now, when it comes to navigating the veteran's healthcare system and the bureaucratic maze to get my conditions acknowledged as service-related, it was an ordeal in itself. It's as if my battle didn't end with my service; a new kind of warfare unfolded, requiring me to validate my suffering to the institutions I served. This unwarranted cross that I had to bear, unfortunately, is a shared struggle among many veterans who find themselves in a similar predicament, seeking acknowledgment and assistance for the sacrifices that continue to exact a toll long after their service has ended. The journey through this systemic labyrinth can feel incredibly lonely, as if I'm on trial, compelled to prove the authenticity of my pain and the legitimacy of my claims.

Was it worth it?

    At the end of the war in Afghanistan, a conflict that felt like both a lifetime and a moment left me wrestling with questions about the impact and the legacy of our involvement. I thought about the goals we'd set out to achieve and the lives irrevocably altered in the process both at home and abroad, and wondered, 'Was it worth it?' This question lingers, hanging in the air like the last note of "Taps" at a military funeral. The silence that follows offers no answers.

The truth is, there is no perfect time to stop fighting and leave a country. However, this truth doesn't make the aftermath of war any less painful. Despite the progress made, women's rights in Afghanistan have been rolled back to the levels they were at before 2002, which feels like a slap in the face. The abrupt exit in Afghanistan left many of us with the same question.

Was it worth it?

Was it worth it for me to lose seven months without my family, loved ones, and more importantly, not seeing my daughter? Time is precious; losing so much time and witnessing our results diminish overnight can be devastating. Yet, amidst these unanswered questions, I can say this: just as in some instances in life - even when you fight a good fight, there are things beyond your control. My skilled disposition was to learn how to pivot, adjust and focus on the new norm.

In wrestling with the unanswered questions about the worth of our actions and the impact of our sacrifices, I found consolation in the community of others who shared these burdens with me. Together, we sought meaning in a world that our service had irrevocably changed, even if the transformation wasn't immediately visible. My eight-year tenure in the U.S. Army, equally divided between active duty and the reserves, was an unanticipated voyage of self-discovery. It went beyond the discipline and the missions—it was a timely instrument used to navigate the emotional aftermath of choosing placement for my daughter's adoption and seeking a new direction amid the whirlwind of my emotions. The military environment honed my ability to focus under duress and taught me to compartmentalize my personal life from my duties.

Reflecting on my military service and its aftermath, I grapple with a mix of emotions—pride, frustration, sorrow, and a sense of acceptance. The scars I carry, both visible and invisible, are a testament to a journey fraught with trials but also imbued with significant growth. It's a chapter of my life that for better or worse built a different type of resilience. Despite the obstacles, the frustration, and the ongoing battles for recognition and care, I sincerely wouldn't exchange this part of my life for anything. It has endowed me with a unique perspective on life, the value of service, and the profound strength that emanates from navigating through and rising above life's trials. It is a significant epoch in my personal development. It has taught me the importance of advocating for oneself and those who have walked similar paths. My military service, with all its highs and lows, remains an integral part of my narrative and continues to influence my journey.

The sight of the U.S. flag, once a simple symbol of the country evolved into something profoundly personal after my military service. It transformed into memories, each star and stripe weaving stories of sacrifice, honor, and loss. Suddenly, the flag wasn't just a national emblem; it was faces I knew, voices I remembered, and the silent stories of countless families forever changed by service. Each flutter in the breeze felt like a whisper of those stories, a silent salute to the bravery and the ultimate sacrifices made.

This indelible image stays with me—a mother clutching a folded flag close to her heart, the only tangible piece left of her soldier. It's a heart-wrenching reminder of the true cost of service, measured not in medals or accolades but in empty chairs at dinner tables, missed birthdays, and memories that will never be made. This image reshaped my view of Memorial Day and other patriotic holidays. They shifted from occasions of communal celebration to moments of introspection, reflection, and a deep-seated frustration at the disconnect between the celebratory atmosphere and the solemn realities these days represent.

Chapter 9:
Transitioning

Transition:
changing or shifting during a period that will cause transformation...

After the military, life was no walk in the park. I expected life to slow down, but it felt like I had hit fast-forward and landed straight into unfamiliar territory. Suddenly, I was no longer the person who could run for miles before dawn or complete an impossible obstacle course with ease. The body I had once trusted had become a sort of frenemy – I was plagued with pains and limitations that I hadn't seen coming. Looking back, I want to grab a time machine, punch in the date of my military heyday, and pause life right there. But reality doesn't come with a remote control, and I had to face it—my tune had changed, and the rhythm of my life was now something I barely recognized. Trying to re-establish myself in a world not governed by orders and regimented schedules wasn't easy either.

With all the highs and lows of service and the transition back to civilian life, this journey continues to unfold. The person who once wore the uniform is not the same one who now navigates the civilian world. Coming to terms with this change wasn't instantaneous. A new form of self-discovery and acceptance was on the horizon. As with such, new paths that led me through various roles and experiences began to unfold. Each lesson taught me something vital about myself and acclimating to the world around me. The realization that I was fundamentally altered was both unsettling and liberating. It dawned on me that adapting didn't mean losing my identity but expanding it to embrace the complexities of my experiences.

This process of acceptance was coupled with the

necessity of learning to be kind and to offer grace for the moments when the weight of my past felt too heavy to bear. It was about understanding that healing is not a linear process and that setbacks are part of the journey forward.

This wasn't about missing the action or the bonds but about grappling with what I felt like was a foreign body with a different agenda than my own. Getting acclimated to it again involved many doctor's visits and adjusting my expectations.

> "....it took eight years of continued neglect and placing the mission, or anything else, above me..."

Every day, it felt like I was navigating through a fog, where every step forward was tentative and filled with the anticipation of either a breakthrough or another setback. My body failing me did not happen overnight; it took eight years of continued neglect and placing the mission, or anything else, above me while overlooking every other aspect, including my health. My back was one example. I remember it like it was yesterday: I injured my back during an obstacle course exercise and got sent to the doctor. The doctor prescribed muscle relaxers and ibuprofen and gave me a referral for physical therapy. On my first scheduled day of therapy, I had field exercise to do. Therefore, I did not get the chance to return to the prescribed treatment afterward. This became the pattern during my time in the military. Making sure I was healed was over-sighted to my commitment to be a present soldier. It was literally the physical manifestation of my internal struggles - put the pain on the back burner and move forward. In this case, the notion that purpose would outweigh it did not work. Not all injuries you can leave unhealed to heal itself over time.

My health situation and the job market made me feel like a fish out of water, the water being a mirage in the desert of opportunities that appeared just out of reach. I pounded the pavement and sent out resumes like they were going out of style, yet the silence from potential employers was deafening. I felt my military skills, which I wore like badges of honor, were suddenly invisible to civilian eyes. In many cases, employers who replied often told me,

"You are not the most qualified."

This is another way to say, "Yes, you are qualified, but I do not want to hire you." This hunt for a decent job became my new mission, albeit without the clear objectives or bond guiding my military days. The job search became a marathon but I ached for my connections in the service. My battle buddies, who could understand a sigh over the phone as a thousand unspoken words, were now scattered across different paths, facing their own transitions. The parts of my life that I put in the sea separating us while I was deployed and stationed far away were drawn back into view once again.

Back home my family tried to bridge the gap in understanding. There was a gulf between us, widened by experiences they could not fully comprehend because of their lack of full knowledge. Despite being surrounded by people, the loneliness felt like a constant shadow, a silent companion that wouldn't leave me alone. This disconnection seeped into my relationships with old friends, too. In an attempt to catch up with high school acquaintances, I realized our worlds had diverged so much that finding common ground felt like an archaeological dig. Their conversations about the latest local gossip or job promotions felt distant, almost foreign. It wasn't their fault. How could I expect them to comprehend the weight of silence in a war zone or the strength of bonds formed in the face of danger? My lens on life had shifted, coloring my perspectives with shades they had never seen.

In this maze of readjustment, I stumbled upon the harsh truth that the sense of purpose that had once been my north star in the military was now obscured by civilian clouds. Job opportunities felt out of reach, and the respect or recognition I had earned in uniform seemed nonexistent to those who hadn't shared my experiences.

What NOW....

It felt as though my sacrifices were invisible. The structure and clear-cut goals I was accustomed to were replaced by an open-ended question...What now? It was a question that echoed in the empty spaces of my days, a reminder of the uncertainty that now framed my existence. But, I decided: No more aimless wandering! I began to pick up the pieces slowly, but it was steady and intentional. I started by embracing the small things – a morning run that didn't aim to break records but to clear my head, picking up hobbies that had nothing to do with productivity and everything to do with joy.

I started learning the art of patience, not just with myself but with life, understanding that healing and adapting take time and can't be rushed. I started cherishing the small wins, like making it through a day without pain being the first and last thing on my mind. I found new ways to stay active that didn't demand as much from my body but still kept my spirit ignited.

Slowly, the job rejections became less of a verdict on my

worth and more of a redirection, guiding me toward opportunities that valued the unique blend of skills and perspectives I brought to the table. I realized that my military experience was not just a list of duties performed but my adaptability, leadership, and qualities that eventually led me to a job where I felt both employed, engaged, and appreciated.

   Securing my undergraduate degree in criminal justice was a milestone and a tangible representation of my determination to forge a new path. Yet, education was just one piece of the puzzle. The real challenge lay in finding a place where I fit in the civilian job market, a task that led me through a series of roles, from cashiering to becoming a sterile processing technician and, eventually, a traveling sterile processing technician. Each position offered new insights, from the mundane to the profound, and helped me build a rewarding and challenging life. Traveling for work brought financial stability and a sense of adventure but also masked an underlying truth—I was running. Moving from state to state, hospital to hospital, I avoided confronting the deeper issues, the mental and physical tolls that demanded attention. The military mindset of pushing through pain and masking vulnerability had become second nature, a survival mechanism that served me well in service but less so in civilian life. Years had passed in this way - a blur of work and superficial healing, until the world came to a standstill with the onset of a global pandemic. During this forced isolation and reflection time, I made a significant life decision—I purchased my first home. While a cause for celebration, this milestone also served as a mirror, reflecting the parts of myself that I had been too busy to confront. The intense emotions tied to my decision to place my daughter for adoption, feelings I had assumed time would fade, reemerged with striking clarity.

The quiet of the pandemic, the stillness of being in a place solely mine, stripped away the distractions and left me with my thoughts, regrets, and hopes. The joy of homeownership was intertwined with a deep sense of introspection, a realization that no amount of physical movement could outrun the need for mental and emotional reckoning.

While I became adept at masking pain and moving forward, true healing requires facing the past, acknowledging the hurt, and allowing myself the space to grieve and grow. In the silence of my new home, in the middle of a world paused by the pandemic, I found the courage to start this process, to seek the help I had long deferred finally. It's a step toward not just surviving but thriving, a recognition that while the military taught me to be strong, true strength lies in vulnerability, in the willingness to confront my pain and embrace the complexity of my journey.

As I journeyed through life, mental health, which was once a foreign concept to me, became a crucial aspect. It provided me with the strength to confront everything and helped me grieve the emptiness that was left after the adoption. It also allowed me to forgive myself for my decisions at 19 when I had nothing and knew nothing. Throughout this season of transition, some moments felt like I hit rock bottom. But one thing about that disposition is the only way left to go is up. All I knew was that life could not go backward. I had to move forward. At last, my faith became fortified.

Reflecting on this journey, I realized that the sense of purpose I thought I had lost was evolving, finding new expressions and avenues. The loneliness, the disconnection, and the aimless days were all part of the process – they were necessary chapters in a story far from over. This tale of transformation is a reminder that even in our most solitary moments, we are not alone in our experiences. Every step, no matter how much we might falter to take it, is a step toward finding our way home, a place where we can rest and be at true peace. As I contemplate the road ahead, I appreciate the lessons learned and my faith increasing. This chapter closes not with definitive answers but with a commitment to continued exploration, healing, and building a future that honors all parts of my story—the triumphs, the losses, and everything in between.

When I found out I was unexpectedly pregnant, I thought my life was over. Everything I had planned, all the goals I had worked so hard to reach, felt like they were slipping away. It was overwhelming, and I couldn't see a way forward. But what I thought would be the end of my life turned out to be my saving grace. Using the placement process of adoption of my daughter was the hardest decision I've ever made, but it was also the one that changed me the most. The raw emotions that came with that choice forced me to shift my entire perspective on life. I had to dig deeper into myself than I ever thought possible, and in the process, I grew in ways I never would have pursued otherwise.

I became someone I never imagined I could be stronger, more resilient, and more determined. The woman I am now, the one who can weather storms and embrace challenges, didn't exist before. My daughter gave me the strength to find her, and for that, I am forever grateful.

Despite it all during this season, my daughter became my saving grace.

Chapter 10 :
Knowing my why

    The onset of the global pandemic, COVID-19, while a crisis of unimaginable scale, brought with it an unexpected pause in the constant motion of life—a forced stillness that provided me with a chance to confront the ghosts that had long haunted the corridors of my mind. For so long, I had mastered the art of classifying, neatly tucking away the most painful parts of my past, like the heartbreak of what felt like losing my daughter to adoption. But as the world slowed down and the distractions faded, these suppressed emotions demanded my attention, refusing to be sidelined.

    In the quiet isolation of my home, the issues I had shelved away for "later" stared back at me, unavoidable and urgent. It was a confrontation I knew I could no longer defer. The pandemic, in all its disruptive horror, strangely became a catalyst for a personal reckoning that was long overdue. I realized that to move forward, I had to go back, to dive into the unresolved pain that I had allowed to fester in the shadows.

Deciding to seek professional help was a pivotal step. It wasn't an easy decision. Admitting the need for help initially felt like a personal failure, given my military background, where resilience often meant stoicism. Yet, reaching out for support became one of the most courageous things I could do. It was an acknowledgment that healing was not just a matter of willpower but a complex process that required guidance, expertise, and support beyond well-meaning friends or family.

Therapy began as an exploration of the layers of grief and guilt that I had wrapped around the memory of my daughter's adoption. Each session was a step towards untangling the intricate web of emotions I had woven over the years. The guilt of not being there for her, the grief of missing out on her milestones, and the sorrow of the 'what-ifs' were all laid bare. These were not easy conversations; tears, long silences, and moments of overwhelming sadness often punctuated them. However, as exhausting as these sessions were, they brought clarity. Discussing my feelings with a therapist helped me see how my experiences had shaped my perceptions and reactions to the world around me. It was revealing to understand that my habit of compartmentalizing was not just a military-bred trait but a survival mechanism that had its roots deep in the trauma of my past. This insight was both a relief and a challenge—it offered a path to healing and rebuilding my emotional landscape.

The pandemic, while a period of global loss and uncertainty, ironically provided a private space for evaluation without exploitation. Being in this safe space by myself allowed me to revisit my past with a new perspective that was less about judgment and more about understanding and forgiveness. I learned to extend the compassion I offered to others so freely to myself, recognizing that healing was not a betrayal of my strength but an enhancement of it.

Evidence of faith, planted in me from my early years of childhood, began to sprout and provide comfort as I returned to spiritual practices in the rituals and prayers that were once pillars. This spiritual reconnection was not about finding all the answers but about seeking comfort in the presence of God, acknowledging that some wounds are too deep for human hands alone to heal. I fought my own battles within the four walls of my home as the world outside was battling the pandemic. This was a period of introspection and hard-won gains in self-awareness and mental health. Revelations were not only about coping with past pain but also about equipping myself with the tools to deal with future stress more healthily. As I embarked on this new chapter, the notion of being the best version of myself took precedence.

The decision to use the placement process of adoption for my daughter was at the forefront of my life for all those years afterward. The choice echoed daily of what I gave up willingly. This decision was not made lightly, and I was determined not to let it be in vain. I wanted to bring honor to that choice. I knew I needed to strive for success, not just in my career but in my well-being. I understood that to move forward truly, I had to put my health first, addressing the aspects of my life that had long been neglected. I realized this while the world was at a standstill, which gave me a rare opportunity to pause and reflect.

Admitting that I needed help was a pivotal moment. In my mind, grieving the void of my daughter was not permitted because I brought it on myself. I decided to place her up for adoption; therefore, I viewed the aftermath and

> "If other single mothers could manage, why couldn't I?"

pain as a small price to pay. I told myself that if other single mothers could manage, why couldn't I? This harsh self-judgement was compounded by my family's ignorance of not only my pregnancy but her birth, her adoption... and her entire existence. The burden of this secret added layers of isolation and guilt to my struggle.

As vulnerability became my strength, I finally took the monumental step to open up to my family about my daughter. It involved breaking down years of built-up walls and challenging the deeply ingrained cultural norms that dictated silence over open dialogue about personal struggles. In the Haitian community where I was raised, mental health was rarely discussed, often dismissed, or misunderstood as a weakness or an ailment that could be prayed away.

Seeking therapy was another significant step in challenging the cultural stigma associated with mental health care. It was a decision that went against everything I had been taught about keeping family matters private and handling issues within the home. Yet, recognizing the necessity of professional help was crucial for my healing process. Therapy provided a safe space to unpack the deep-seated feelings of guilt, loss, and inadequacy that had plagued me for years.

Although the pandemic was still technically in effect, the world carefully opened back up, allowing some positions to start back in office. Upon returning to work, I was thankful for the structured environment provided by a government position. It still involved serving and protecting. This return to a disciplined, orderly setting helped me regain a sense of purpose and stability. While in other areas where I was unraveling and needed the space to release and be undone, the value of the career choice gave me a reminiscence of the structure that I needed. It was the perfect balance for recovery and growth.

As I was pulling together the pieces of my new normal, there were things that I knew I would need. Reintegrating into "church life" was one of those pillars that I felt necessary for wholeness. I needed community again. As in the military, the crucial support and connection got us through some dark moments. This season, community meant having people around who believed as I did and could walk through this process of personal upheaval in a healthy, progressive way. As I was finding my stability in re-establishing the foundation of my faith, prayer guided my reflection. This spiritual revival was not just about seeking forgiveness or understanding but about nurturing a relationship with God that I had neglected in the busyness of life. He had to become my source. Believing in my faith reassured me that forgiveness was my portion. Healing from this stance of understanding meant that I could acknowledge that the emotions I had buried deep within, tied to the adoption of my daughter, fed me the lie that I had no right to mourn because the loss was a consequence of my own choice. This self-imposed silence was a heavy burden I carried each day with stoic resolve, believing that to feel sorrow was to admit fault unforgivably.

With faith and therapy, my eyes were opened to a different truth that liberated me. It taught me that grief does not discriminate between the choices we regret and the ones we celebrate. It touches us all, regardless of the circumstances that invite it into our lives. I learned that mourning the loss of my daughter to adoption wasn't an indulgence in self-pity but a natural human response to an unexplainable deep loss. It was a necessary process, a way of honoring the depth of the bond we shared, even briefly.

    This realization did not come easily. It was the product of many therapy sessions, filled with tears and the kind of honest self-reflection that can feel as painful as it is healing. In those moments of vulnerability, I faced the hard truths about my decisions and their impact on myself, my daughter, and everyone else involved. Understanding that it's okay to grieve—that there's no shame in feeling sad or expressing pain—was a turning point. Sometimes, we make choices under duress or from places of necessity. We can find compassion for those who have to make choices from this place. As an afterthought, when we are no longer in that place, we can feel delayed sorrow, which is followed by the haunts of what we could've done differently. These decisions underscore our humanity. My capacity in that season of life to make a complex, emotionally driven decision reflected the depth of my feelings that no matter how I may have messed up, my engrained morals proved that I still had the innate ability to do what was best for another person, even if she wasn't born yet. It wasn't her fault, and because she existed, she deserved a well-lived life. While actively pursuing healing, I found strength in sharing my feelings with others, particularly those who had walked similar paths. It helped to alleviate the isolation that had compounded my grief. I was not alone in my experiences. With time and patience, I am continually growing into the acceptance that it all had a purpose and that everything worked for the good of us all.

    As much as I would love to say that the therapeutic process was linear and straightforward, I cannot. It involved setbacks and days when the grief felt as fresh as it did in the beginning. Each step forward, no matter how small, was a piece of the puzzle in rebuilding a life marked by compassion for myself and a deeper appreciation for the complexities of human emotions.

North Dakota.....

    My new career choice meant having to be assigned to different areas. All roads led to North Dakota, where my first government assignment post-military life awaited me. At first glance, this placement felt like another twist of fate's cruel humor once again. I found myself in a freezing climate, a stark contrast to the tropical warmth of my youth. Initially, I resented this relocation; it felt like yet another separation from everything familiar and comfortable and notably far from my family and the life I had started to rebuild. However, as I settled into the quiet of North Dakota, I began to see this isolation was not a punishment. It was yet another phase of personal assessment for growth. It was as if the universe, or perhaps divine intervention, had orchestrated this moment of solitude to force me to confront the things I had been avoiding. With the pandemic closing off usual social escapes and delaying plans, the question posed seemed clear,

    "Are you ready to deal with your past?"

    North Dakota's vast serenity and unhurried pace provided calmness. The vast plains and harsh weather mirrored the starkness I often felt within, providing a transparent backdrop to project my thoughts and fears without distraction. The experience of being in North Dakota was genuinely transformative, and it helped me discover a new level of buoyancy that I never knew existed within me. As I would walk through the cold, often lonely streets of my new city, I pondered how in isolation, I didn't feel "alone". I was understanding the core of who I was. It was a paradoxical experience—feeling alone yet deeply connected to the universe and my purpose.

My residence became more than just a living space; it transformed into a place of introspection and healing. The physical unpacking of boxes mirrored the emotional unpacking I undertook. Each item I placed and each picture I hung felt like a step to understanding and accepting the complexities of my past decisions. With the support of my therapist, I delved deeper into the emotions surrounding the adoption of my daughter. Those sessions, often through virtual meetings due to pandemic restrictions, became lifelines. They helped peel back the layers of guilt and grief that I had wrapped tightly around my heart. I was guided through the process of recognizing my decision rooted in selflessness, although painful, had provided a beautiful, loving, and stable life for my daughter.

Seeing her thrive had always been a silent reassurance. This young lady who was growing up with opportunities and happiness, through every update provided, was my saving grace. She was a testament to the power of tough, loving decisions that parents often have to make for their children's well-being.

Concluding this chapter of my journey, it's crystal clear: my daughter is the linchpin of my motivation, the driving force behind every decision, every effort, and every instance of perseverance in my life. From the moment I made the heart-wrenching decision to place her with another family, ensuring her future and well-being has been the underlying current of my every action. Reflecting on the sacrifices and the paths chosen, I recognize that she is why I strive for success in everything I undertake. The thought of her grows stronger with each challenge faced and each barrier overcome.

Living without her physical presence is a daily challenge, but our bond transcends the conventional norms of proximity. It's a bond forged in the deep desire for her to have a life filled with love, opportunity, and happiness—a life that I envisioned for her from the moment I knew of her existence. She is "my why"! I push through difficult days and continually seek to better myself. In every role I assume, whether professionally or personally, the underlying motivation is to make her proud and to someday share with her the story of my life, with all its complexities and triumphs, and to show her that every decision, especially the tough ones, was made with her best interest at heart.

Her influence extends beyond the personal realm into my professional life. She inspires me to uphold integrity and commitment in my duties because these values are what I hope to pass on to her. She is the silent observer in all my actions, the unspoken judge of my choices, and the joy that lights up the darker moments. I see parts of myself in her—through updates, pictures, and stories shared by her adoptive parents. Each glimpse into her world is a reminder of why the struggles were worth it. She thrives, and in her thriving, I thrive.

Every step forward in my life is taken with her in mind, hoping that when she's old enough to understand, she'll see the tapestry of sacrifice, redemptive love, and determination that her existence inspired. For her, I've learned to rise after every fall, learn from every failure, and embrace each success not as a personal victory but as a stepping stone toward providing a legacy she can be proud of.

Thus, as this chapter closes, it's not just a reflection on what has been but a reaffirmation of my ongoing commitment. My daughter is why I continue to evolve, why

I face each day with renewed purpose, and why, despite the physical distance, I remain ever-present in her life. She is my greatest motivation, the beacon that guides my choices, and the love that sustains my spirit. Everything I do, I do for her, fueled by the hope that one day, our paths will intertwine once more in a story of reunion and shared futures that could only be beyond my wildest dreams.

Though stretched over miles and mediated by the context of adoption......

this connection remains unbreakable and is the cornerstone of my resolve.

Chapter 11: Limitations

October 2nd, 2023

"This morning, as I lay here in my Calgary home, it's clear that physical pain isn't just a fleeting visitor; it's more like a stubborn tenant that is deeply entrenched in every part of my body. I woke up feeling like I'd been run over by a bus. My back, legs, thighs—every joint screams as I try to move. It's a weird mix of emotions: I'm proud but also really in pain. Despite the pain, I successfully completed a 10k running race. But there's another ailing feeling – a deep, gnawing kind that comes from knowing what this pain represents—the years of service, the physical toll it's taken, and how it's shaped my life choices, including the tough decision about neglecting my health.

Mornings are tough, but they're also a chance to prove that I can do this. My reality, however, is every morning I wake up, I'm reminded that I'm no longer the healthy 23-year-old I was when I joined the military. It seems my body is now deceiving me; I often hear that I look young, but my body aches tell a different story. As in every day, today is not about enduring but finding small victories within the routine, the daily humdrum. The challenge lies in finding strength amid adversity, weaving together hurt and pride, and creating a narrative of endurance and recovery."

This narrative is the consistent realization that since stepping away from active duty in the military, my body has become a constant battleground of discomfort and pain. It feels like my body is gradually giving up on me. Daily pain is my new norm; my lower back seems perpetually inflamed, and despite numerous attempts—physical therapy, chiropractic sessions, and dry needling—relief remains elusive. To get through each day, I've come to rely on muscle relaxers and ibuprofen, a regimen I never imagined would become my lifeline.

It wasn't like this in my days in uniform, where I was conditioned to push through pain and to view it as a temporary obstacle rather than a constant companion. Now, it feels as though the strength and stability I once took pride in are being tested in ways I never anticipated. The physical demands of military life have left a lasting imprint, and the transition to civilian life has not provided the relief I once hoped it would. The deeper realization of the toll that service took on my body. The presence of pain is not just a physical symptom to be managed but a signal of deeper issues that need addressing. It's a reminder of the sacrifices made, visible only to those who bear them. This acknowledgment doesn't make the pain any easier to feel, but I chose to reframe it within a context of honor and sacrifice, a narrative I hold close to the most demanding days.

In this new reality, the small wins give me peace of mind. On days when the pain is more manageable, I feel a surge of triumph, a brief return to the person I used to be. I cherish these moments, which remind me that despite my physical condition, my inner strength is still intact. Doing so motivates me to seek solutions and not give in to pain. I've come to understand the importance of my mental strength. Just as my body requires care and attention, so does my mind. Recently, I have developed a habit of focusing on mindfulness and breathing techniques. I use these tools to cope with the frustration and fatigue that chronic pain can cause. While these practices don't erase discomfort, they provide mental clarity that helps me deal more effectively. Connecting with others who have experienced similar things has also been imperative to keeping things in perspective. I still keep in touch with a few battle buddies. These connections are a lifeline, offering both practical advice and empathetic support. These interactions remind me that I am not alone in this struggle—others have also navigated the difficult transition from the structure of military life to the uncertainty of civilian life.

    I am learning to redefine my strength, not as the absence of vulnerability but as the courage to confront and adapt to it. Each day, with each minor adjustment, I am slowly crafting a new way of being that honors both my past service and my current reality. Running is my new highlight of perseverance! The unique feature on my running app has become my lifeline on many days - "I need a win run". Despite doctors advising me to hang up my running shoes for good, arguing that it might be the cause of my relentless pain, it remains my way of clearing my mind. It's the one thing that brings clarity and relief when life's pressures mount. Running isn't just a form of exercise for me; it's a determining coping mechanism. Something I find that brings peace and happiness. Whenever I feel overwhelmed or like I'm failing, lacing up my sneakers and hitting the pavement offers a temporary escape from those heavy feelings.

    The "I need a win run" from my running app is a tailored experience that understands what I need in those challenging moments. Besides building endurance or speed, I am choosing with my body in every stride to overcome the mental and emotional hurdles that weigh me down. Some days, I concur that the run is the only victory I experience therefore, the idea of not running ever again is unbearable. Recently, I decided to test my limits further by signing up for a 10k with the Calgary Police Run. It was more than just a race; it was a personal challenge, a way to prove to myself that my circumstances would not defeat me. I could still achieve something significant despite the ever-present pain.

On the day of the race, I was filled with a complex mix of anticipation and apprehension. The excitement of finally reaching this moment was undeniable, yet it was overshadowed by the fear of whether my body could hold up under the strain. Each kilometer was a battle, not just against the physical distance, but between my sheer determination to finish and the discomfort that gnawed at me with every step. The pain threatened to overwhelm me at times, but the thought of crossing that finish line—of proving to myself that I could push through—kept me going. With every passing marker, I reminded myself that this race was more than just a test of endurance; it was a symbol of my resilience, a chance to show myself that despite the setbacks, I could still move forward. When I finally crossed the finish line, it felt like a personal triumph, a victory not just over the race but over everything that had tried to stop me. But it came at a cost. The aches and fatigue settled in, a harsh reminder of the toll it took. The aftermath was brutal—my entire body ached, and simple tasks like climbing stairs became almost impossible feats. I spent the whole day after the race lying on the couch, unable to move.

I learned a hard lesson that day about listening to my body. Yes, I finished the race, but realizing I had pushed myself too far overshadowed the victory. Muscle relaxers, ibuprofen, and salt baths, which usually helped soothe the pain, were no match for the aftermath of those 10 kilometers. The pain made me question whether the run was worth it. But there was a glimmer of something else. Was pride the culprit? Although I had faced my fears and not let them control me, I was reminded me that my body, while not as resilient as it once was, still had fight left in it. I had hoped that maybe with the proper training, I could get back to tip-top shape, but I wasn't there yet.

I understood that my relationship with running needed to adapt. I wasn't giving up, but I had to find a new way to continue doing what I loved without compromising my health. This meant setting more realistic goals and being okay with slower paces, perhaps finding alternative ways to stay active that were gentler on my body. The thought of walking at a steady face pace while I nursed myself back to health could be just as instrumental. As I move forward, I'm learning to balance my love for running with the need to protect my health.

When I enlisted in the military at 23, I was the epitome of health. I had never seen the inside of a hospital for any ailment of my own. I imagined the military would be physically demanding, so, ironically, I imagined challenges would be more about endurance than lasting health effects. Yet here I am, years later, and it feels like every bit of that early resilience has been chipped away.

I remember stepping into the military full of vigor, ready to tackle whatever challenges came my way. The physical demands were intense, sure, but my body coped admirably. I could handle long runs, heavy packs, and sleepless nights —the typical grueling routine didn't faze me. Looking back, the accumulation of years of demanding physical activity and the stress of military life began manifesting in ways I hadn't anticipated. The minor aches and pains you shrug off as part of the job. But as time went on, these minor nuisances became constant, evolving into chronic conditions that no amount of medication seemed to alleviate completely.

The irony is that the very institution that built me up, instilling a sense of invincibility, has also been a catalyst for my physical decline. While frustrated at my body's betrayal to be as vibrant as my youthful days and nostalgic for unbridled strength, there is this sobering, inevitable resignation to my new normal of limitations. The military trained me to push through discomfort, ignore pain, and prioritize the mission. But that mentality has drawbacks in civilian life, where listening to your body and taking care of your health hold a different weight for the longevity of living. I've had to learn, often through trial and error, that ignoring pain isn't a virtue—it's a risk.

Moreover, it is essential to note that the Veterans Affairs healthcare system presents unique challenges. My struggle to have my conditions recognized as service-connected was a nightmare. Nevertheless, it is the only way to secure the necessary treatments, and dealing with the bureaucracy of veteran health services can feel like a second job. Fighting for proper care is exhausting, adding a layer of stress that only exacerbates my ailments.

Reflecting on the past few years, I marvel at how much I once managed to juggle simultaneously. There was a time when I could work two jobs, pursue a college degree, and handle the demands of pregnancy, all while maintaining an appearance of balance. I remember being able to sleep in brief snippets, anywhere and anytime, recharging with my little downtime before springing back into action. That version of me seems like a distant memory now, as managing just one job feels like all I can handle today.

My current reality is a far cry from those days of endless

energy. It's a battle that consumes significant energy. What used to be dedicated to my career and studies now serves as a detailed and slow process, filling out paperwork, long appointments, and the constant need to prove the impact of my military service on my health. This fight for recognition and appropriate care is draining, both mentally and physically, and it underscores a harsh reality many veterans face. The narrative that veterans are well cared for post-service often feels more like a well-polished myth than the reality in which I live.

Sleep has become another casualty in this battle. Where I once could operate on a full night's rest, I now find myself functioning on about three to four hours of sleep per night. However, despite my physical limitations, I completed my master's degree—an achievement that, under these circumstances, feels monumental. Yet, realizing my current limitations tempered the joy of this academic accomplishment. I've learned to adjust my expectations and redefine what success looks like. If before I measured achievement by how much I could do, now I gauge it by how well I can manage each day's tasks without compromising my health. It's a quieter, less visible form of forte, but no less significant.

Chapter 12:

Now What

Mirline DORT

SA SE KOWEN

> *"Now faith is the substance of things hoped for, the evidence of things not seen."*
> *— Hebrews 11:1*

In this verse, I am reminded that I don't have to have all the answers because I serve a God who knows everything. I will remain hopeful when things seem dark and bleak because the sun will come up in the morning, and He holds the reigns. It has taught me the power of maintaining a positive outlook while patiently waiting for God's timing. Throughout my journey, I've come to realize that waiting isn't a bad thing but rather a time of renewal. It's a period for reflection, growth, and adjusting my mindset. One of my favorite songs, "Wait on the Lord," deeply resonates with the season I'm in right now. It reminds me that there's a purpose in the pause.

As for my recent achievement of completing my master's degree, this milestone holds a lot of significance because I suffered a tremendous amount of pain during the last semester, the worst I've felt since leaving the military. It took me five months to find answers; each doctor's visit resulted in a different diagnosis and new medication and surmounting attempts at home remedies from well-meaning family and friends. My sleep was scarce, ranging from 2-3 hours at night while giving my best at work and schoolwork. Even in my exhaustion, I kept pushing because I could see the finish line ahead. There is more to this degree than academic success. It is another representation of resilience to set out to achieve something despite the situation and circumstance.

Today, my life is about more than enduring pain and

overcoming physical challenges. It's about making every day meaningful and impactful. I approach each morning with a plan to manage my limitations and maximize my capabilities.

My narrative as an immigrant kid isn't just about where I've been; it's also about where I'm headed. With faith guiding me and a renewed sense of purpose, I am ready to face the future, whatever it may bring. My story is one of continual growth, learning, and hope, driven by the unwavering belief that there's always more to strive for. As long as I am here, I have a purpose. It may shift in how this purpose reveals itself and what impact is made, but I'm flexible to understanding that with each season, I am who God created me to be unapologetically!

I've come to realize the importance of being kinder to myself. It's a lesson in patience and understanding that has reshaped my daily routines and how I respond to my body's needs. Instead of pushing myself to run, which has long been my way to cope and clear my head, I've started embracing the gentler walking rhythm. This shift might seem small, but it significantly changes how I treat myself. My goals are no longer driven by pride but by a compromise between maintaining my health and honoring my love for staying active.

Yet, learning to rest, truly rest has been another crucial step. I used to associate staying in bed with laziness, a belief rooted in my upbringing, where it was practically unheard of to remain in bed in our household. As my only day off was Saturday, I had to help my mother deep clean the house, and Dad didn't understand the concept of sleeping while Mom cooked and cleaned. Now I understand that some days, the most productive thing I can do is allow my body to recover. Resting doesn't mean I'm lazy; I'm giving myself the care I need to function better in the long run. As I care for my body, I pace my understanding of how I respond by learning about how to effectively handle emotional triggers. In the past, painful memories and decisions, like the adoption of my daughter, would surge up unexpectedly, and my immediate reaction would be to find something to occupy my mind. I would have brushed these feelings aside in the past, as I was conditioned not to allow myself to feel or process them. Now, I give myself the grace to fully feel these emotions, understand them, and learn from them without judgment. This approach has helped heal old wounds and made me kinder and more compassionate towards myself and others.

Embracing kindness towards myself has broadened my understanding of self-care. It's not just about occasional treats or indulgences but about consistently listening to my body and respecting its limits. It's about replacing self-criticism with self-compassion, recognizing that every step back or moment of rest is part of a more significant journey toward wellness.

This transformation has not been instantaneously overnight. It's a daily effort to remind myself that it's okay to slow down, to acknowledge that my pace now might be different from what it once was, and that's perfectly fine. Each day brings challenges and learning opportunities, and I'm getting better at listening to what my body needs from me. The impact of this gentler approach extends beyond physical health; it influences my mental and emotional well-being. I find that my world has expanded in beautiful, unexpected ways. My relationships are more profound, my days are more fulfilling, and I'm more in tune with the person I am becoming.

Rebuilding and deepening my relationships with my family has been one of the most important chapters in my life. This reconnection has healed old wounds and enriched my life in ways that have provided me with the best of both worlds. I am fulfilled, and my bonds with some of my older and younger siblings have been strengthened as I allow them to get to know me, not the shell that I created for protection.

    Rekindling these relationships began with candid communication channels that had long been neglected. I decided to intentionally set aside past grievances and misunderstandings. I had to approach each conversation with openness and vulnerability, ready to listen and to forgive. The more I understood and forgave myself, the more I could extend that forgiveness to others. I can honestly say that mending my relationship with my parents has been one of the most rewarding experiences of my life, especially with my mother. Our conversations are endless; sometimes! I get off the phone two hours later without remembering what we discussed, but I feel lighter afterward.

    The joy of these renewed family ties is multifaceted. There's comfort in knowing I have their support and love, just as there's joy in knowing I can reciprocate. I look forward to family gatherings filled with laughter and shared stories. Each occasion adds a level of intimacy and understanding, strengthening the fabric of our family. Moreover, this reconnection has provided stability and support, which has been necessary as I navigate my health challenges and the complexities of everyday life. Knowing I have a network of people who genuinely care and understand me adds strength and confidence to my daily endeavors. Reflecting on this aspect of my current state of belonging fills me with gratitude. It reinforces the idea that no experience was wasted. Every difficulty has the potential to lead to growth and renewal, both within oneself and in relationships with others.

The twists and turns of my journey, each challenge, laugh, tear, and triumph, have shaped who I am, weaving a rich tapestry that tells a story of strength and grace. Every obstacle I've faced has been a lesson in disguise. Life hasn't always been straightforward. There were days when everything felt overwhelming, especially the decision to place my daughter for adoption, a choice that echoed through every corner of my being. But this lifelong process of moving forward, no matter the odds, shows me I was graced for this life, every last part.

The lighter, simpler moments often brought unexpected joy and relief. Those clear skies that presented breaks in the storm reminded me that life isn't just about enduring. There are moments when you can find joy in the every day, no matter the weather. These experiences helped to balance the tough times, making the journey not just bearable but also beautiful in its complexity. I've seen how every experience, good or bad, has been a step on the path laid out for me. Recognizing God's hand guiding each step lets me know my life is not in vain. It's shown me that a bigger plan at work uses every part of my story—from the trials to the triumphs—to forge a stronger, more compassionate me. The relationships I've nurtured along the way—family, friends, and even brief encounters—have enriched my life immeasurably. They've taught me about love, sacrifice, and strength found in community. These connections have been my anchor, offering support and understanding through every season.

My past, with all its complexities, has prepared me for whatever lies ahead, imbuing me with the right tools, wisdom, and a deep-seated hope for the future. As this chapter of my life closes, I see it not as the end but as a stepping stone to new beginnings. My experiences empower and ready me to face the future with a renewed spirit. The narrative of my life is one of continuous evolution, driven by a deep faith and a steadfast determination to improve, not just for myself but for my daughter and everyone whose life I touch. It's about transforming adversity into strength and finding meaning in every experience.

So, as I move forward, I do so with a heart full of gratitude and eyes open to the endless possibilities that await. My journey is far from over; in fact, it feels as though it's just beginning. With the right tools, a heart full of faith, and a spirit ready to soar, I literally believe the sky is the limit! I am well equipped to reach for it, no bars held. I carry a renewed sense of purpose underpinned by the profound truths found in Psalm 144:1, KJV:

"Blessed be the Lord my strength which teacheth my hands to war, and my fingers to fight..."

Beyond words, this is the bedrock of my walk with God, a guiding light that has illuminated my path through the darkest times. It has been a source of strength and assurance, especially during moments of challenge and self-doubt. Each time I'm faced with the challenging task of weapon qualification—a test that measures more than just my ability with a firearm—I rely on this verse for strength. Reciting it with my mother, feeling the weight of each word, instills in me a sense of invincibility and calm. It's a ritual that transforms my nervous energy into steadfast courage, ensuring I never falter when it counts.

This, along with other scriptures, has fortified my spirit and reshaped my understanding of what it means to be a believer. They remind me that my capacity to overcome is not just about enduring but thriving, drawing strength from a well of spiritual depth that never runs dry.

Unwritten Chapters awaits....

Now, as I stand ready to embrace life, I am not just surviving but THRIVING! With every challenge I've faced, I've gathered tools and insights that equip me just as a GPS would for the unknown road ahead. The setbacks that once seemed impossible have become testimonies of my strength and adaptability.

I want to leave you with a clear message:

I'm not done yet.....

With unshakable faith, I am poised to succeed. The impossible became possible. This isn't just a story of a little shy, intimidated Haitian immigrant girl overcoming; it's a story of transformation and perseverance. Every step forward is propelled by the certainty that my path is ordained, that every challenge is an opportunity for growth, and that my journey is far from over.

Through this book and my life story, I want to convey a sense of determination and optimism through the experiences that I went through. Let these words resonate not as an end but as a promise of continued growth and boundless possibilities. The story of my life, enriched by each verse and trial, continues to unfold in a beautiful, relentless love story of gratitude and expectation, and I am living life...Sa Se Mwen.

About the Author

Mirline Dort: Born in Haiti in 1986, Mirline grew up as the eldest of four children in a close-knit household with her mother and stepfather, whom she gratefully calls her dad. From her biological father's side, she is the youngest of 15 siblings. Her life took a dramatic turn at the age of 12 when her family immigrated to the United States, marking the beginning of a remarkable journey. Central to her story are four foundational pillars: faith, community, education, and family.

A combat veteran with eight years of service in the United States Army, Mirline has demonstrated a lifelong commitment to public service, continuing her career for more than a decade after her military tenure. She holds an associate's degree in Surgical Technology, a bachelor's degree in Criminal Justice, and a master's in Criminal Justice Management. Her dedication to protecting the homeland is not just a job but a profound passion.

Though her work often requires her to be stationed in remote locations, Mirline always makes time for her family and loved ones. In her downtime, she loves traveling to new destinations, going for brisk jogs, hiking through scenic landscapes, and relaxing with a good book.

I'd love to Stay *Connected*

Social Media

@authormirlinedort

Email

mirlinedort@gmail.com

Website

https://mirlinedort.com

The Lovejoy
PUBLISHING CO.

www.ingramcontent.com/pod-product-compliance
Lightning Source LLC
Chambersburg PA
CBHW050913160426
43194CB00011B/2391